Refugeed

Exodus Poems

Reginald Flood

Refugeed

Copyright © 2018 by Reginald Flood

All rights reserved. No part of this publication may be reproduced, stored in a retrieval system, or transmitted in any form, or by any means, electronic, mechanical, recording, photocopying or otherwise without the prior written permission of the publisher.

Editor: Randall Horton
Cover art: "1815 Dated Charleston South Carolina Slave Tag." Private collection, www.bridgemanimages.com
Cover design: Red Ghost

ISBN 978-0-9992232-8-4
LCCN 2018935199

Willow Books, a Division of Aquarius Press
www.WillowLit.net

Printed in the United States of America

For
Gary Wayne Flood
When it gets hard, I still can hear your laugh

Contents

Prologue..9

Narrative by Henrietta Ralls...10
Driving Lesson After Dreaming Mamie Till Discussing Ferguson......11
Introduction to WPA Interview Questions...13

I..15

Stealing Prayer...17
Wood Pile...18
No Hoodoo...19
Carving...20
Empty Pretty Land...21
Winter Vultures...23
WPA Transcription of Interview of Sallie Crane..................................24
Biscuit Dirt...25
Natural Causes...27
You Could Live..28
WPA Transcription of Interview of Lulu Jackson................................29
Ash Cakes and Silence...31
Smith's Cove at Low Tide...32
New Onions, Old Scars...33
Before First Nor'easter of Season..34
Early Moon Gourd...35
Ritual..37
WPA Transcription of Interview of James Graham.............................38
Before Cotton Sacks and Cabins...39
June Twilight...41
One Ear and Half a Face of Scars...42
Editor's Notes on Dialect by Sterling Brown......................................44
Porches...47
Questions (Part 1)..48
Instructions..49
WPA Transcription of Interview of Ellen Cragin................................50
Questions (Part 2)..51
Note Pads and Handkerchiefs..52
Questions (Part 3)..53

II..55

Bad Feet..57
Where Angels Still Dance..59
WPA Transcription of Interview of Ellen Brass...........................65
Walk on a New England Beach After the Mansion Tour..........68
Back Brace..69
Suet..80
After Church..81
Let The Good Times...82
Good Deal..83
WPA Transcription of Interview of Silas Dothrum...................84
Middle Aged in Montego Bay..88
Camouflage..89
Clean...90

III...93

No Shotgun..95
Sledgehammer Goodbye..96
Junkyard Lace..98
Undertaker's Aria..100
Salt and Fear..101
Leather..103
Double Fat and Fries..104
Pork Fat and Sorrow..105
Bedpans and a Pretty Box...107
No Stooping...109
Blood and Metal Flake Blue...111
Writing Nightmares...112

Epilogue...115

Traffic Stop..117

Acknowledgements...119

Notes...121

About the Author..124

refugeed

To convey slaves away from the advance of the federal forces

Prologue

Interviewer   Bernice Bowden
Person interviewed   Henrietta Ralls
                       1711 Fluker St.
Age   88   Pine Bluff, Ark.

"Yes ma'am, I was here in slavery times. I was born in Mississippi, Lee County, March 10, 1850. Come to Arkansas when I was ten years old. Had to walk. My old master was Henry Ralls. Sometimes we jump up in the wagon and he'd whip us out.

"My old mistes name was Drunetta. She was good to us. We called her Miss Netta. Old master was mean. He'd whip us. One day he come along and picked up sand and throwed it in my eyes. He was a mean old devil. He thought I was scared of him. Case I was. That was before the war.

"I recollect when the Yankees come. I knowed they was a'ridin'. White folks made me hide things. I hid a barrel of wool once - put meal on top. They'd a'took it ever bit if they could have found it. They wanted chickens and milk. They'd take things they wanted - they would that. Would a'taken ever bit of our wool if they could have found it.

"They wouldn't talk to old mistes - just talk to me and ask where things was. She didn't notice them and they didn't notice her.

"I reckon the Lord intended for the Yankees to free the people. They was fightin' to free the people.

"I hear em say war is still goin' on in the world.

Driving Lesson
After
Dreaming Mamie Till Discussing Ferguson

1. *Mamie Till*
Ellis Island will always be the easy lie
that's why I opened my boy's box to let folks
see burnt up history cut and wrapped in barbed wire
so they could see what it was to *survive on sadness*.

I listened to Billie a lot, Ella too, but mostly Billie
after the whole damn city filed by one-by-one
to see what they left of my boy. 100,000 people
one-by-one walked by his beat up and burnt up body.

The trip down south to sit in that stuffy courtroom
and hear them lie about my boy was hard. He
was a good boy, and just looking at that white lady
straight in the eye shouldn't have gotten him killed.

Jury. Nine white men. 67 minutes. I knew what they
were going to do, we all knew what they going to do.

2. *Father*
Son, you know where everything is: turn signal,
brake on your left, accelerator on your right
put the key in ignition—nah don't turn it on
we need to practice something first. Keep your hands

on top of the wheel, then extend left hand out the open
window while the right hand slowly eases out the keys.
Nah, that's too fast, go slow, go easy. Keep the left
extended. Don't shake. Now extend the right hand

out slow to match the left, gently drop the keys
on the blacktop. Move right to open door. No
slower, a cop will be telling you this, you just follow
his directions. No. Hell no! Slower than that, no jerky

movements, nothing sudden, step out one
foot at a time — palms out, hands in the air.

3. *Mamie Till*
I feel real sorry for his mama — the way they let
him lay in the street, four hours without a sheet:
nothing. I understand now that they want you to see.
Same with Emmett, the barbed wire wrapped round

an old tire to his body — them white men just wanted
him in the water a while — let it ruin his face
those men weren't scared of getting caught
they knew nothing, nothing was going to happen.

30 days after the verdict the magazine paid them
4000 dollars, four thousand to tell exactly how they took
my boy, how they beat him, how they burned him
before they shot him in the head and dumped him

in the Tallahatchie. I don't know about that policemen,
don't know why he did it, but why did that body lay there?

4. *Father*
I know you're eighteen, I don't care how this makes
you feel. This is the first lesson about driving,
you going to be in LA, Orange County this summer
you got to know how to be stopped. Yeah. Maybe.

This is probably my own damn baggage, but it's also
my damn car. I making you what? Internalize your
oppression! Where you get that shit? Listen, I don't
care how you feel about this. I am not asking. I'm not.

I am not going to stand in some room, and look across
a slab with you on it, at your mama's face. You roll the
window down when you see the lights. Slow, everything
slow. I am getting out the car. We going to do this again.

You ain't driving shit until we get this right.
None of my tears are white, none of my tears are white.

11478

WORKS PROGRESS ADMINISTRATION
Federal Writers' Project
1500 Eye St. N.W.
Washington, D. C.

SUPPLEMENTARY INSTRUCTIONS #9-E

To

THE AMERICAN GUIDE MANUAL

FOLKLORE

STORIES FROM EX-SLAVES

Note: In some states it may be possible to locate only
a very few ex-slaves, but an attempt should be
made in every state. Interesting ex-slave data
has recently been reported from Rhode Island, for
instance.

April 22, 1937

11478

STORIES FROM EX-SLAVES

The main purpose of these detailed and homely questions is to get the Negro interested in talking about the days of slavery. If he will talk freely, he should be encouraged to say what he pleases without reference to the questions. It should be remembered that the Federal Writers' Project is not interested in taking sides on any question. The worker should not censor any material collected, regardless of its nature.

It will not be necessary, indeed it will probably be a mistake, to ask every person all of the questions. Any incidents or facts he can recall should be written down as nearly as possible just as he says them, but do not use dialect spelling so complicated that it may confuse the reader.

A second visit, a few days after the first one, is important, so that the worker may gather all the worthwhile recollections that the first talk has aroused.

Questions:

1. Where and when were you born?

2. Give the names of your father and mother. Where did they come from? Give names of your brothers and sisters. Tell about your life with them and describe your home and the "quarters." Describe the beds and where you slept. Do you remember anything about your grandparents or any stories told you about them?

3. What work did you do in slavery days? Did you ever earn any money? How? What did you buy with this money?

4. What did you eat and how was it cooked? Any possums? Rabbits? Fish? What food did you like best? Did the slaves have their own gardens?

I

……..The reason they kept her was they had refugeed her children off to different places to keep them from the Yankees. They couldn't get them back.

Lucretia Alexander
Little Rock, Ark 1936

Stealing Prayer

Rachel Fairly, 1936

There was a world of yellow people then.
My mother's sister had two yellow children
from her Master, they were as white as the white children,
after the war they were refugeed to cook and clean
for their brother and sister. There was lots of folks run off like that:
almost white, copper colored, coal black, all rounded up
and herded to Texas before the Yankees came. My cousins didn't
get free for many years, not until after they were twenty.
But there were near white slaves all over
where I was raised up, their mothers were colored —
that made the difference, that's what gave them slave life.

My mother stole all the time, just about everyday
in slave life. She said she had a hard time getting through.
Mostly food because she had to, couldn't get enough
any other way. After freedom she wouldn't touch hogsheads
because she stole it dried and ate it so much.
My parents were sold away from each other
on the same day, but later Mother was given to Father's master
by his sister. Mother had to work the field everyday, even Sunday.
Father was a coachman. The first time I remember seeing him
he wore a big beaver hat and huge old coat for special days
we called the ham beater. He drove and tended the horses.

Mother told me about having to pray under a pot
a big black one she used to cook with in the yard. In summer
slaves cooked outside their cabins or they would burn up.
She told me about finishing the cooking, big mess of rice and mustard greens
mixed with hog jowl pieces she snuck out the smokehouse.
That pot had to feed fifteen people, after eating she cleaned
the pot careful, dumped it over, put her head inside and went to prayer,
everyday this happen, especially after she stole.
She told me about putting her head inside and entering all that darkness
to call God, that's what she would do – open her eyes
to blackness, and raise her voice loud to scream
for Jesus under the cooking pot in the yard, until the echo
got so bad there was nothing left: no breath, no sin, no shackle
sores, just the iron dark suckling her for a minute free.

Wood Pile

At nine degrees metal etched into spine
catches, bent over to pick oak from birch,
red maple from poplar. The first
gunshot echo shocks me back to a brittle time
when bang didn't mean a buck just climbed
gut shot into a brown tangle of honeysuckle

to bleed out. I can't grasp the gone, buckle
each name in my head to stone, flesh, dirt
without thick smell of exhaust and asphalt
stinging eighty degree air in December,
because a sharp breeze, blacktop brined with salt
doesn't let sweat and fingerprints linger

long enough to call out a single face
of the ghosts that refuse peace in this place.

No Hoodoo
                                    Lucretia Alexander, 1936

My mother died at seventy-three or seventy-five.
That was in August 1865. They kept her
because they refugeed off most her children
to different places to keep them from the Yankees.
They never got none of them back.

My papa was sold five times. Some say he lived
to 112 years, others say it was 106, but he ended up having
a long life. He wouldn't take nothing off folks
spent lots of time in the stocks, got whipped raw
in daylight several times. But he still wouldn't take nothing.

I seen some brutish doings by folks: running niggers
with hounds, whipping them until they was bloody,
The whipping was the worst thing, two people
would do it at once—master and overseer so the lashes
fell quick in rhythm until the backs got ragged bloody.

First time I got sprinkled was by a white preacher,
when they sent him to the cabins after he preached
to the white folks it was always the same text,
always the same sermon, serve your masters, don't steal
your master's turkeys, don't steal your masters chickens.

On weeknights my father would have church in our dwelling
house – real church with real preaching, real praying
no difference between Baptists, Methodists back then.
Nobody turned down for communion, nobody shunned out,
just our hymns and prayers done in a whisper.

Them services all I want to remember from slave life
I don't believe in no hoodoo, but under my bed
I keep a white bowl with spring water, mustard seeds
and coriander floating to keep the whip sounds out my dreams
so I can hear clear again the quiet in those prayers.

Carving

Each June spikes on the wild raspberry jut
out razor next to the woodpile, waiting for flesh
reaching for small sour berries that are less
fruit than seed, not worth the quick cut
scribed into this forearm like a plow rut
through ink matching great-grand pop's

mark on bowl or board he made to let rise drop
biscuits that proofed into wonder after rest
under washed burlap. That hand-milled flour
kissed with salt and fresh churned butter
swelled on land he scraped and clawed out the power
to bleed for himself, and not have to mutter

morning anger the burnt red of these feral berries
about a man, a barn and charred flesh he had to carry.

Empty Pretty Land

Doo Quin, 1937

All of the young people I knew back then
have been dead many, many years.
But this white lady on my porch wants to talk
about it, about before the surrender.
What she really expect me to say about filling
a sack? Bent hard and heavy
over a row day after day from first light.

Heard about these folks at church.
Walk in your house with paper, pencil to write
down stories, ask you questions bout slave life.
What am I suppose to say? That I can't see faces
in my head anymore, that I need the scribbling
in that old bible to remember the names of my own kin.
That what I can remember clear is when old Ogburn
lost the place, that slow walk from Mississippi
next to wagons weighed down with what white folks
could save from that life. She don't want to hear
about the hard joy in that, I weren't free yet,
but this place still was a wonder, valley
was one big canebrake; nothing lived in here
but bears, wolves and mean varmints.
But all the ground beneath you was deep, dark
easy to furrow, everything grew up quick,
the whole damn hollow was empty, nothing
but fresh sky jutting down to all this green.

I know she don't want to hear about that,
about all the pretty in an empty land that you knew,
just knew was soon going to welcome you free.
We all knew it was going to come after Cornith
I can't not talk about the killings there that changed
that Mississippi mud for all of them. I can't forget
the fighting: five acre field so thick covered with dead
and almost dead you couldn't touch dirt walking.
War took everything from Col Ogburn after that,
both plantations, horses, cows, two of his sons.

He made a lot of us join up his regiment to tote water,
cook food, clean the camp. After that fight all we did
was bury folks. The onliest way to bury them
all was to cut a deep furrow, lay the soldiers
head to head, and plow the dirt back on them.
It was only the first days that the dead stayed
with you. Didn't know no better than to lay them out
face up at first, have to watch the mud darken
the blank white eyes and cover the mouths twisted
in anger and hurt. But us working the furrows
learned quick, put them in face down. You get used
to handling them bodies, like hog carcasses
or fresh shot deer you need to dress out quick
in the heat. Became like everyday slave life but easier.
I know she don't want to hear that, but no sack
to fill, no weeds between rows to pull, no overseer
shadowing every step. At Cornith we just gather up
all the different pieces torn by the canons, carry them
to the wagon until it was loaded with bodies, half
bodies enough to fill tight a whole furrow.
I do have that noise stuck in my head though,
don't hear it much at night the last few years, but it
still there, yes its still there, that quick sucking sound
flesh made when it hit the reddened mud.

Winter Vultures

Chain gang tight, each bird etches black into a chrome sky,
circling over a marsh brittle with brackish ice.
Frozen cattails form an upright brown vise
between cove and swamp where things go to die
then rot into meaning, because buzzards glide
down hard in December, forcing terns, gulls

to stand in salt mud at the edges for lull
in beak and talon chaos that crushes bone: slices
muscle from cartilage, flesh and fat from fur
until warm carcass becomes carrion
dried blood, flecks of hair appearing in a blur
where hide and tendon just were—a clarion

call from last sand spit between sea, wetlands
to not paw at dead things we don't understand.

30651

Interviewer   Samuel S. Taylor
Person interviewed   Sallie Crane
Age 90, or more   See first paragraph in interviewer's comment for residence

---------- [Whipped from Sunup to Sundown] ----------

"I was born in Hempstead County, between Nashville and Greenville, in Arkansas, on the Military Road. Never been outside the state in my life. I was born ninety years ago. I been here in Pulaski County nearly fifty-seven years.

"I was born in a old double log house chinked and dobbed. Nary a window and one door. I had a bedstead made with saw and ax. Chairs were made with saw, ax, and draw knife. My brother Orange made the furniture. We kept the food in boxes.

"My mother's name was Mandy Bishop, and my father's name was Jerry Bishop. I don't know who my grand folks were. They was all Virginia folks— that is all I know. They come from Virginia, so they told me. My old master was Harmon Bishop and when they divided the property I fell to Miss Evelyn Bishop.

Age

"The first man that came through here writing us up for the Red Cross, I give him my age as near as I could. And they kept that. You know peace was declared in 1865. They told me I was free. I got scared and thought that the speculators were going to put me in them big droves and sell me down in Louisiana. My old mistress said, 'You fool, you are free. We are going to take you to your mammy.' I cried because I thought they was carrying me to see my mother before they would send me to be sold in Louisiana.

Biscuit Dirt

James Bertrand, 1936

Are your people from around here?
Others have said it was white folks
came to ask the questions. My father was bothered
by patrollers regular. He always got out,
went about to see his friends even before freedom:
they would catch him, lash him a bit
then let him go. That was mostly what he told me
from slave times. Oh, and three hundred pounds
of cotton for the men, two hundred for the women
every day. I don't remember what the old man
said about freedom coming, he farmed
with his old Master after the war
that's when the Klan started coming at night
never whipped my father because he was orderly,
but they came to all the Negro homes often.
We was all raised around here – my father too;
He learned shoemaking and passed it on to me
so I never sharecropped, never worked somebody
else's fields, never had any doings with the Klan.
My life has been different.
These callouses, these cracked hands, this bent over back
that all from me, my work, my time. Half of it
isn't from sweat that ended up in somebody elses
pocket. All my older brother and sisters are dead,
they worked the fields from sun up to sun down,
before and after the surrender, don't know how
much freedom mattered in their lives
we never really talked about it. When we got to spend
time on Sundays my uncle would fiddle and we would
sing and dance on the dirt floor of the old man's barn.
It was nice to have the time. I am old
and everything is harder now, but there is work
black folks are hard on shoes, and I got this
little scrap of land to fuss over, the dirt dark and sweet
when I close my fingers around a handful
it stays tight like making a biscuit with fresh
ground flour, and even though my hands ache

from the age and the damp and all the doings
it feels good to open those fingers, and let that mud
sprinkle back hard onto my own land.

Natural Causes

A crow plucks a new-born chick from a cardinal
nest buried in the hurricane bent branch
of a half-dead hemlock. The beast rips the romance
from April—slow, black, casual—
tilts head and opens beak, making normal
witness to the destruction of beauty.

The seasons are unreliable and unruly
after a third friend's death does not dance
to the blurry beat of tragedy. Albert and I
blew through reed after reed at fourteen for a sound
like Tower of Power to make it a lie
our side of Harbor Freeway couldn't get down.

That funk echoes savage leaving middle age
the baritone sax bleat a hard, hard sage.

You Could Live

Salle Crane, 1936

Yes there were whippings, sometimes from sun up to sun down
but remember I am well past ninety. I was born in the midst of it
not at the end like a lot of others living now. The Red Cross man
came through a while ago, he was the first to write us up – told him
everything near as I could recollect it. But I told him ninety,
truth is I'm well past that. I was born in a double log house
chinked and dobbed, didn't have a window and only one door.
My bedstead, chair were made with saw, axe and long knife
all of our house things were made by my brother Orange.
We kept our food in a cold spring in boxes. It was how we lived.

Of course I remember freedom, it was terrifying, I thought they were
going to put us in a big drove to take to Louisiana and sell.
I was born here. I lived all my life here. Slave life was hard here
but you could live, stories I heard from people coming
from down there was bad, very bad. When they gathered us
I cried, like I said I thought it was speculators, going to sell us south
then my mistress said, "shut up you fool, you are free."
I didn't believe her, didn't believe none of it. I got myself ready
for the long march, for a life of hell, I didn't believe freedom.

30607   #682   18

Interviewer   Samuel S. Taylor
Person interviewed   Lula Jackson (supplement) Cf. 30600
                           1808 Valentine Street, Little Rock, Arkansas
Age   79   Occupation   Field hand

- -

Whippings

"Early Hurt had an overseer named Sanders. He tied my sister Crecie to a stump to whip her. Crecie was stout and heavy. She was a grown young woman and big and strong. Sanders had two dogs with him in case he would have trouble with anyone. When he started layin' that lash on Crecie's back, she pulled up that stump and whipped him and the dogs both.

"Old Early Hurt came up and whipped her hisself. Said, 'Oh, you're too bad for the overseer to whip, huh?'

"Wasn't no such things as lamps in them days. Jus' used pine knots. When we quilted, we jus' got a good knot and lighted it. And when that one was nearly burnt out, we would light another one from it.

"We had a old lady named 'Aunt' Charlotte; she wasn't my aunt, we jus' called her that. She used to keep the children when the hands were working. If she liked you she would treat your children well. If she didn't like you, she wouldn't treat them so good. Her name was Charlotte Marley. She was too old to do any good in the field; and she had to take care of the babies. If she didn't like the people, she would leave the babies' napkins on all day long, wet and filthy.

"My papa's mama, Sarah, was killed by lightning. She was ironing and was in a hurry to get through and get the supper on for her master, Early Hurt. I was the oldest child, and I always was scared of lightning.

A dreadful storm was goin' on. I was under the bed and I heard the thunder bolt and the crash and the fall. I heard mama scream. I crawled out from under the bed and they had grandma laid out in the middle of the floor. Mama said, 'Child, all the friend you got in the world is dead.' Early Hurt was standin' over her and pouring buckets of water on her. When the doctor come, he said, 'You done killed her now. If you had jus' laid her out on the ground and let the rain fall on her, she would have come to, but you done drownded her now.' She wouldn't have died if it hadn't been for them buckets of water that Early Hurt throwed in her face.

"Honey, they ain't nothin' as sweet to drink out of as a gourd. Take the seeds out. Boil the gourd. Scrape it and sun it. There ain't no taste left. They don't use gourds now."

Interviewer's Comment

Violent death followed Lula Jackson's family like an implacable avenger. Her father's mother was struck and killed by lightning. Her mother's first husband was thrown to his death in a wrestling match. Her own husband was dragged and kicked to death by a mule. Her brother-in-law, Jerry Jackson, was killed by a horse. But Sister Jackson is bright and cheery and full of faith in God and man, and utterly without bitterness.

Ash Cakes and Silence

Richard Gump, 1936

I am the only one living that I know of
my mother was the mother of thirteen children.
The way things are now I probably won't be here
for long. Only get 4 dollars a month and some commodities
from welfare pension that has to go for food and rent,
it is hard, they cut me down very low, it is hard.
You don't get nothing much when you get commodities
no grease to cook with, no flour, no milk.
Whatever they want to give me I will take it and make out
it's how I live my day to day. If they would send
a slave pension I would take it—I need it.
I got heart problems, high blood pressure, it is hard.

My father was from South Carolina, he knew his people
My mother was from Tennessee, she didn't know hers.
My mother was looked at as a bully. The overseer tried to whip her once
and she wouldn't have it, I remember that, she grabbed a hoe
backed into a corner and dared him to come in.
He didn't go. After freedom we worked shares for a while.
One quarter for cotton, one third for corn
all of us worked the field hard. None of us had time
for school, too much work, too little money. They needed all
of us in the field. Most my brothers, sisters born after slave times
It was a Monday when they came around and told us we were free.
Old marse walked up to my father and said you can stay or go,
you as free as I is, nobody can domineer over you no more.
We left the next day to start working shares.

I shot craps, played cards until I got with the church.
After religion, I don't do none of that.
I remember my mother made real good ash cakes.
When she made them for my daddy she would put a piece
of paper on the top and a piece of paper on the bottom
to keep them clean. After he would finish eating on them
she would let us have what was left. Sometimes when she was mad
mother wouldn't use no paper. Daddy would pick them up, look
and say "no paper today," and mother would shake her head no.
Then he wouldn't say nothing more about it.

Smith's Cove at Low Tide

The wind shimmers bark ice through the tree
line, a brown sweep of woods meeting brittle
December sky, and there are only little
glories left: vultures, gulls on a rocky half-frozen sea
picking at new carrion too cold to bleed,
unlike wounds from the unsorted dead

I can't mend with all the words left unsaid
from those old stories that succor middle
age, but this winter takes a hard share:
joints ache, the bottle calls, and blurry specter
of spoon, needle hover just outside the tender glare
that brightens handful of years left with her,

while the buzzards, gulls pull at frigid bones
for heart, liver, lung among salt and stone.

New Onions, Old Scars

Henrietta Ralls, 1936

I hear em say war is still going on in the world.
And now this white lady outside
walking up to my little porch with yellow paper, pencil:
heard from Quinn about these folks,
they want you to talk about before the surrender,
bout cotton, cane, hunger and all that -
but they don't want to know bout the hardness of it.
Not going to talk bout all the nastiness,
no white folks want to hear that.
Miss Netta's dead but her people lives
just cross the bridge and up the hill.
She weren't that bad, but old master Henry
was a devil, when we came from Mississippi
I was just ten years old and had to walk all the way,
he would whip us out the wagon
then throw salt and sand on the welts.
Don't think bout slave life much,
can't say what's there to say—remember it more than I want,
back hurt bent over washing tub
fingers tied into knots that shot needles to bone.
When I cook or sew now, I want quiet
like my mornings, scrape in this little garden
for a bit, cut some collards and mustard
pick tomatoes and new onions for supper
while air still wet, before the sun raises up so hard
stooping in my own dirt feels like working a row.

Before First Nor'easter of Season

The beagle's yelp carries hard, sharp and clear
in eight degrees. The still, ripe air gobbles
up the sound of that hound, and I can't coddle
the departed anymore, can't translate fear
into small steps to make this day, this week, this year
a totem to fight the small crises of the flesh

each bone ache, each muscle strain, each thick breath
invites because it is hard to swallow
burnt salt and sorrow, hard to watch a single gull
against a gray-chrome sky fly away from the sea.
Two years until sixty, and I can't cull
the memories, toss aside ones that still bleed

or hold close the healed to patch the fissure
between sleep, flesh, and the coming blizzard.

Early Moon Gourd

Lulu Jackson, 1936

They sent a black man to hear my stories,
he out there in the center of the cabin
sitting at the table close and comfortable, hard to believe.
But should I tell the truth? Should I?
Should I say how death follows all my years?
When I say it all out loud it sounds like a lie.
My papa's mama struck by lightning, my mama's
first husband thrown to death wrestling,
and my own man kicked to death by that damn mule.
Sounds like lies.
Like things old folks make up so they
don't have to talk about the real damnation
during slave times. At first he might not believe
my master's name: Early Hurt,
that was his God-given name. But they still a lot
of Hurts up and down this hollow,
so he can probably take that in.

I remember my sister, how she would fight
that Satan of an overseer Sanders, how that one
time he tied her to the stump to whip her or worse.
After Crecie pulled up that stump she beat him
and both them mean dogs he walked around with.
Master Hurt had to come whip her himself,
he wasn't happy with nobody, cussing and screaming
at both of them. Only Crecie could do that.

I wish I could forget that day lighting killed
my papa's mama. I see it too clear some nights
the way they laid her out on the floor and poured
bucket after bucket of cold water on her, until they finally
got the doctor: he said they killed her quicker
she might have been okay if they just let her be.
She was the only friend I had in this world.
Still know all the things she taught me
how to use a pine knot for a lamp,
how to weave reeds into a tight basket,

how to make a sweet water drinking
gourd. I remember us out in the garden picking
the best shaped gourds, had to look close as possible
to the shape of an early moon.
Then we would scrap them out careful
boil them good and dry them out hard.

Does he really care about any of this?
Or is this just his relief check? He got paper
pencil getting ready to write what I say,
but does he really want to hear about all this?
Water still taste sweeter out of one of those gourds
like a little bit of rest for a moment,
to this day I feel hard the sudden taste of it.

Ritual

The finches fuss in the grass ice for seeds
worms frozen by rain that turned mean,
fifteen degree drop since dawn casts a crystal sheen
two inch thick on wetland mud and dead reeds.
"Son, this some Arctic shit, its time to grieve"
the old man walking his Doberman at noon

yells with a limp toward Smith's Cove and dunes
pockmarked with snow and piss that won't freeze.
You fucked up again. Totaled truck, half consumed
bottle, plastic handcuffs and same slurred
phone call I can't understand, covering wounds
that won't scab with grimaces and grunts for words

that just signal a cage instead of a slab
where blood and flesh might settle the tab.

30690

Interviewer Samuel S. Taylor
Person interviewed James Graham
408 Maple Street, Little Rock, Arkansas
Age 75

["Free Negroes"]

"I was born in South Carolina, Lancaster County, about nine miles from Lancaster town. My father's name was Tillman Graham and my mother's name was Eliza.

"I have seen my grandfathers, but I forget their names now. My father was a farmer. My father and mother belonged to this people, that is, to the Tillmans.

"On my father's side, they called my people free Negroes because they treated them so good. On my mother's side they had to get their education privately. When the white children would come from school, my mother's people would get instruction from them. My mother was a maid in the house and it was easy for her to get training that way."

Before Cotton Sacks and Cabins
Mattie Aldridge, 1936

They ain't nary a drop of white blood in none of us.
My pa was born in Mississippi. He belonged to the Duncans
He was named George Washington Duncan.
I can't hardly remember getting free. Papa
came from the field and just said, we don't have
nothing, but we going leave off of here.
I do remember Grandma. She'd tell stories about old times
about before cotton sacks and cabins. Grandma
never did talk plain, she couldn't tell things straight,
used strange words and mixed up language.
Talk about animals, trees you would never see
in Mississippi, you couldn't tell what she say most the time.
She knew candle burning and root healing. I liked hearing
her talk, been so long I've forgotten a lot.

Pa was a field hand, mama was a house girl.
they was glad when freedom happened, their white
folks was hard on them. Whooped them. Hurt them
beat them all the time. Pa was killed in Arkansas
clearing new ground. Signs mean something in this world.
A storm came up quick and a big limb hit him,
killed him where he stood. I still think about him
all the time. Grandma and ma always told us
when you build a house put in all the windows
you want – it bad luck to cut a hole and add one.
Sign of death. Day before that limb flew Papa put
a new window in the cabin. Mama came home
stared at it, then started lighting candles, but it was too
late, Pa was already in the field. The folks with him
say the log came spinning through the air
took his head right off. White man running the crew
said it was just an accident, didn't mean nothing, after they found
his head he made everybody get back to work
or lose pay for the whole day. But how do you account
for his face, eyes wide open and mouth tight lipped
like he knew what was happening, like he was thinking:
first slave life, then half freedom, now this, like he knew.

I ain't got no business telling you this. Nobody wants to read this. White folks don't believe in signs.

June Twilight

The bat furiously flies in circles too early
too early in twilight, no shadows yet to shield
it from a Cooper's Hawk that just makes one more kill,
fur, leathery wings, crushed into a blurry
bundle of talons, bat flesh in a deliberate flurry
that's missing from the last moment of most life.

The six years you've been gone have been rife
with things to share: the end of middle age yields
hesitant magic: ache-free spine, sweet potato flowers,
humid afternoons freeing arthritic fingers
to sop up pepper shrimp and okra with sour
dough bread that lets the sweetness linger

on a tongue cloistered with heat from an old recipe
that scents the air with stories that still bleed.

One Ear and Half a Face of Scars

James Graham, 1936

I know I have seen my grandfathers
at least once but the faces are blurred now
they were both stooped over a clay berm
separating a rice field and creek ditch
waist deep in muddy water in the South Carolina sun.
They were both coal dark thin natural Black
men. Everybody said both were born across the ocean.
My mother said when they spoke sometimes
the words made no sense, but each knew everything
about rice, how to make dirt dams hold
for the season, when to drain or fill a field,
when the stalks would be ready to thrash.
On my father's side they called my people "free negroes"
because master Graham treated them so good.
They didn't dress in burlap, had corn flour
not just coarse meal and got learning.
My mother's side had to sneak reading
from master's kids when they came back
from school. She was a maid in house
that was how she got her training.
What I can remember most about slave times
is folks hip deep in mud and dark water,
women and children flailing stalks
until you felt like your arms would fall off,
and my aunts weaving baskets in mud-thick heat.
My mother's name was Eliza, my father's
name was Tillman, they stayed together
all their lives. I don't know if I want
to remember more, but those two old men
their faces straining; one with a shovel
the other with a pick axe working on that dyke
should be clearer to me, I know one was missing
an ear, the other had scars running down
half his face, but I should be able to see
them clearer, even in this old mind
I should be able to trace out the shape
of their faces, that would be better,

instead of thinking back on it
and just seeing all that mud.

<u>Notes by an editor on dialect usage in accounts by interviews with ex-slaves. (To be used in conjunction with Supplementary Instructions 9E.)</u>

Simplicity in recording the dialect is to be desired in order to hold the interest and attention of the readers. It seems to me that readers are repelled by pages sprinkled with misspellings, commas and apostrophes. The value of exact phonetic transcription is, of course, a great one. But few artists attempt this completely. Thomas Nelson Page was meticulous in his dialect; Joel Chandler Harris less meticulous but in my opinion even more accurate. But the values they sought are different from the values that I believe this book of slave narratives should have. Present day readers are less ready for the overstress of phonetic spelling than in the days of local color. Authors realize this: Julia Peterkin uses a modified Gullah instead of Gonzales' carefully spelled out Gullah. Howard Odum has questioned the use of goin' for going since the g is seldom pronounced even by the educated.

Truth to idiom is more important, I believe, than truth to pronunciation. Erskine Caldwell in his stories of Georgia, Ruth Suckow in stories of Iowa, and Zora Neale Hurston in stories of Florida Negroes get a truth to the manner of speaking without excessive misspellings. In order to make this volume of slave narratives more appealing and less difficult for the average reader, I recommend that truth to idiom be paramount, and exact truth to pronunciation secondary.

xxix

I appreciate the fact that many of the writers have recorded sensitively. The writer who wrote "ret" for right is probably as accurate as the one who spelled it "raght." But in a single publication, not devoted to a study of local speech, the reader may conceivably be puzzled by different spellings of the same word. The words "whafolks," "whufolks," "whi'folks," etc., can all be heard in the South. But "whitefolks" is easier for the reader, and the word itself is suggestive of the setting and the attitude.

Words that definitely have a notably different pronunciation from the usual should be recorded as heard. More important is the recording of words with a different local meaning. Most important, however, are the turns of phrase that have flavor and vividness. Examples occurring in the copy I read are:

    durin' of de war
    outman my daddy (good, but unnecessarily put into quotes)
    piddled in de fields
    skit of woods
    kinder chillish

There are, of course, questionable words, for which it may be hard to set up a single standard. Such words are:

    paddyrollers, padrollers, pattyrollers for patrollers
    missis, mistess   for mistress
    marsa, massa, maussa, mastuh   for master
    ter, tuh, teh   for to

I believe that there should be, for this book, a uniform word for each of these.

The following list is composed of words which I think should not be used. These are merely samples of certain faults:

1.	ah	for	I
2.	bawn	for	born
3.	capper	for	caper
4.	com'	for	come
5.	do	for	dough
6.	ebry, ev'ry	for	every
7.	hawd	for	hard
8.	muh	for	my
9.	nakid	for	naked
10.	ole, ol'	for	old
11.	ret, raght	for	right
12.	snaik	for	snake
13.	sowd	for	sword
14.	sto'	for	store
15.	teh	for	tell
16.	twon't	for	twan't
17.	useter, useta	for	used to
18.	uv	for	of
19.	waggin	for	wagon
20.	whi'	for	white
21.	wuz	for	was

I should like to recommend that the stories be told in the language of the ex-slave, without excessive editorializing and "artistic" introductions on the part of the interviewer. The contrast between the directness of the ex-slave speech and the roundabout and at times pompous comments of the interviewer is frequently glaring. Care should be taken lest expressions such as the following creep in: "inflicting wounds from which he never fully recovered" (supposed to be spoken by an ex-slave).

Finally, I should like to recommend that the words darky and nigger and such expressions as "a comical little old black woman" be omitted from the editorial writing. Where the ex-slave himself uses these, they should be retained.

This material sent June 20 to states of: Ala., Ark., Fla., Ga., Ky., La., Md., Miss., Mo., N. C., Ohio, Okla., Tenn., Texas, Va., and S. Car.

Porches

Interviewer Four, 1936

They never expect me. I always get
that raised eyebrow, quick second glance,
then a slow, slow smile. Most the women
offer lemonade, ice tea or cool water on the porch
to escape the heat, none of them expect
to talk about their slave life with a black man.

I know they were forced to hire me, state folks
in Little Rock do not care if negroes
talking to negroes gets more truth, once these good folks
understand I'm not from relief; that talking to me
won't risk their check or raise problems with kin
of white folks used to own them, words are easy.

The struggle to learn steno was a blessing
these marks have never been put to better profit
this yellow pad, this pencil lets me get it all so I can
record more than words, get at truth in a world
that wants to forget their sweat, their faces,
so I sit comfortable in their dirt yards, on their porches

and we just talk about what they remember.
I take down each story the way it should be told
slow and clear in their words; however they tell me
sharpened by anger, fogged by sorrow; the marks
on this yellow pad must echo everything,
the sour in these lemons, the sting in this chipped ice.

Questions (Part 1)

Where did slaves sit in church?
Were slaves allowed to have pencils?
Did slaves ever fight with poor whites?
Were there ever slave dances?

Who preached to slaves?
Were slaves allowed to handle books?
Did poor whites ever beg from slaves?
Describe the way slaves danced?

Were slaves allowed to own a bible?
Did slaves have secret "learning lessons"?
What did whites call free Negros
What music was there at slave dances?

Did slaves mourn for dead mistress or master?
Did slaves mind being called nigger?

Did slaves mind being called nigger?
What were the types of winter clothing?
Were newborn slave babies good looking?
How far were the quarters from the mansion house?

Where were slaves sold?
What were the types of summer clothing?
Were newborn white babies good looking?
What size was the mansion house?

What was the attitude of slaves to being sold?
What did slaves do when it rained?
Have you been happier in slavery or free?
Was the mansion house pretty?

Did slaves clean their shoes on Sunday?
Did slaves use grease or lard on their hair?

Instructions

Interviewer Four, 1936

I need to make their words clear so someone
will listen. Douglass did not write the way slaves
spoke, Booker T did not record his story
in the language floating above cabin floors
and the big house. Nobody hears this bondage. Nobody
hears the chains echo and the cotton sack drag
down the rows in these lives. On porches,
at supper tables, on cut stumps in the yard
between cabin and table garden these voices
tell a hard story wedged between relief checks,
commodities and a little scrap of ground
most scratch out nothing more from than supper.

Mr Brown knows the problem isn't "truth to
idiom instead of truth to pronunciation." He knows
the problem isn't deciding to write "snaik" or snake,
"mastuh" or master, "whi fulks" or white folks
but whether you care about what you hear
about getting it right and true while these words
can still be wrenched from this thick Arkansas
air that swirls slow and deliberate over
cotton and hog stink, masking stories about us all.

Interviewer   Samuel S. Taylor
Person interviewed   Ellen Cragin
                815½ Arch Street, Little Rock, Arkansas
Age   Around 80 or more

[Escapes on Cow]

"I was born on the tenth of March in some year, I don't know what one. I don't know whether it was in the Civil War or before the Civil War. I forget it. I think that I was born in Vicksburg, Mississippi; I'm not sure, but I think it was.

"My mother was a great shouter. One night before I was born, she was at a meeting, and she said, 'Well, I'll have to go in, I feel something.' She said I was walkin' about in there. And when she went in, I was born that same night.

"My mother was a great christian woman. She raised us right. We had to be in at sundown. If you didn't bring it in at sundown, she'd whip you,-- whip you within an inch of your life.

"She didn't work in the field. She worked at a loom. She worked so long and so often that once she went to sleep at the loom. Her master's boy saw her and told his mother. His mother told him to take a whip and wear her out. He took a stick and went out to beat her awake. He beat my mother till she woke up. When she woke up, she took a pole out of the loom and beat him nearly to death with it. He hollered, 'Don't beat me no more, and I won't let 'em whip you.'

"She said, 'I'm goin' to kill you. These black titties sucked you, and then you come out here to beat me.' And when she left him, he wasn't able to walk.

Questions (Part 2)

Did slaves use grease or lard on their hair?
Did they maim slaves?
Was there jealousy between house servants and field hands?
Did slaves have a funeral wake?

Were there sex relations between slaves?
Was there jealousy between light and dark slaves?
How did slaves get to be house servants?
Did slaves have a funeral sermon?

Were there sex relations between slaves and whites?
Was there a difference in working hours in the field or the house?
Did slaves have a casket or coffin?
Did slaves resist owners or overseers?

Where was the slave graveyard?
Do you think being a slave hurt the Negro?

Do you think being a slave hurt the Negro?
Did slaves ever sit down in the presence of whites?
What did slaves do on Sunday?
What did free Negroes call themselves?

Did slaves have a ring or broomstick marriage?
Did whites attend special slave services?
How did free Negroes earn a living?
Are times as good now or better compared with slave days?

Was there a mammy for the big house?
What did the preacher take as text for slaves?
What were the regular slave vacations?
Did free Negros get along better than slaves?

Did slaves get time off for a honeymoon?
Did you long to be free during slavery?

Note Pads and Handkerchiefs

Interviewer Four, 1936

This is righteous work. The Lord's work. No hymns,
no chalice, no wafers, just pencil and steno pad
to record words washed in sweat and trial.

This porch swelters, even with Sister Alexander's
lemonade, my forehead, my fingers stain this frayed
handkerchief, each wipe keeping these familiar marks

from smudging into silence. This piece of cloth
is from my mother, the dirt softly clumping on her coffin
forced me south away from that Indiana cold

to thick Louisiana air filled with a language I needed:
privileged to breathe with all those that did not
leave, living each day with cotton and bloodstains.

This history from Sister Alexander is tangled
in pain and confusion: *"Agnes, will you follow me if I buy
your husband,"* words from a mistress passed down

from her mother as the only legacy from a life of kitchen
and field. Fifteen hundred dollars to buy
a twice-escaped slave to join a couple in shackles:

seven decades later Sister Alexander's lilting voice
dry eyes still reflect the raised scars and the wonder
on her father's back and in her mother's voice.

Questions (Part 3)

Did you long to be free during slavery?
Were slaves suppose to tip their hats to whites?
Did whites and negroes sing the same songs in church?
Where did slaves go to the toilet?

Did slaves use the mansion house front door?
Did slaves sing freedom songs?
Did you ever hear of Nat Turner?
Did men and women have separate toilets?

Did slaves assemble at times just to sing?
Did slaves walk alongside their master when together?
Did you ever hear of John Brown?
Did Whites and Slaves have separate toilets?

Did slaves ever own watches, rings, false teeth?
How did you first learn you were free?

How did you first learn you were free?
Did slaves practice Voodoo?
Can you describe the slave sales?
Did you see Mulatto or near-white babies?

Did any slaves cast or break spells?
Where were the slave auctions blocks?
Were there babies commonly thought to be the Master's?
How did you address whites after freedom?

Did you ever see any ghosts or spirits?
What was the attitude of slaves toward being sold?
Did the old folks ever talk about Africa?
Did you ever hear of any white slaves?

Were Negroes allowed to carry a gun after freedom?
Did you see the stars fall?

II

They used to come to my place in droves. Wagons would start coming in in the morning and they wouldn't stop coming in till two or three in the evening. They'd just be travelin' to keep out the way of the Yankees…..

Campbell Armstrong
Little Rock, Arkansas, 1937

Bad Feet

The crackling sound of cedar
burning issues from each big toe.
Hurt knifes from joint to heel
taunting memories of an easy stride
destroyed by pork fat and whiskey.
Now, the mats, sparring gear
smelly Gi in the morning and pain
mocks you for waiting half a century.
    One found stroked out
in his green house, the other in the river
floating near his fly rod: these stories
are not about somebody else's life now
but the failed flesh of friends
that left holes in the world which can't
be covered by clever allusions
and shrewd metaphors.
    This will not be another poem
about growing old, no more rhythmic
whining about joints that throb,
itchy shaved head to hide the gray,
back brace to mow the lawn,
or stiff lean against wall, bed, door
each daybreak to bend into fatigues
two decades from being deep green.
    Pop used to work on his feet
each night after miles with
the mailbag, soaking them in water
so hot he would winch before
rubbing them down hard with oil
and warm rag. With an old
steak knife, worn file he would chop
and hone arches to toes until
corns, calluses and busted blisters
could slip back into those shoes
to night school, second job
with a gait that didn't show any age
    I refuse to walk careful
and flat-footed toward the rocking

chair, toes to arches frozen
in a surrender you can see with each step
toward that damn card table
weighed down with dominos and last lies
of old men jabbering together to forget
the women that are gone, the kids
that don't come by and the ache
each time those squares slam
the table echoing what little remains.

Where Angels Still Dance
Korea Town (April 29, 1992)

i

He walked up to new Honda old man in traffic
stopped in what was a tunnel of fire
removed the nine millimeter, pushed classic
Raybans back on nose, aimed and fired.

First shot in left cheek out mouth, second graze
Adams's apple; third, side of head above
temple, taking a chunk of skull that made
gray hair specked with what looked like red mud.

Before slipping Sig into belt he grasped
car door with left hand, blue tear drop tattoos
on each ebony finger, pulled clasped
prayer beads from mirror with right: blue

white, pink smoothed by rubbing against pale
yellow palms that now echo a muted wail.

ii

One hour after news from Simi Valley
a drive-by every ten minutes,
cheap brass clattering concrete, street to ally
invisible in all the smoke that grimaced

the stucco; signs in English and Korean,
storefronts with metal grating half down
so they could return fire and lean
back behind barrel, old freezer, mounds

of broken cinderblocks from stacks
thrown from trucks, flatbeds, minivans
cruising "K town" looking to crack
some head for that little girl's hand

blown apart rubber banding her braid
by store owner insisting she had not paid.

iii
Why can't I say? Why can't I say? No words
will come out. No words. I remember
elbows, knees, blood marking hurt crawl to curb
palms stinging as they pressed on embers

sprinkling asphalt. There is daughter-in-law
she looks scared, I hope son is not at store,
nothing but smoke and trouble. Did I fall?
Now I remember: gun, man, seatbelt, car door

smell of tires face down on the black top
daughter looks scared; how did I get here?
What are all theses tubes? What is this hard throb
above my ear? I was just trying to steer

around the trouble. I don't want to stay
here, why can't I say, why can't I say.

Avalon Blvd. (August 11, *1965*)

iv
I know my boy ain't perfect but they beat
him bad, real bad - wasn't no reason, none-
so I got my brother and went back to street
where hog tied, I couldn't hardly see my son

in that bloody swollen man on the ground
but I recognized the clothes and hard moan
rising up off black top each time they pounded
him again: then the bottle, then the stone -

piece of brick hit car to make police cower
quick, before they stood back up more mean
than ever, coming at us with clubs and sour
smoke that closes up your throat, making it seem

like you ain't breathing without hurt ever again,
and my boy shouldn't pay for all this sin.

v
Niggers, just niggers, especially those this side
of Avalon, drive in from the Valley to this shit
every damn day, like Nam, except no pride
of country in this, just shoveling shit

so decent folks in LA can do their business,
between blacks here, Mexicans across the river
half the city a cesspool, got no interest
in nothing but drugs, drink and a sliver

of pride in their heritage. I just police them
savage; like this black boy we had to beat
with his momma watching: blood, bile, phlegm
oozing before asphalt helped him to sleep

between nightstick and mace, and now this crowd
chanting, circling into a colored cloud.

vi
Damn! Can't cover my head. Got me cuffed
still beating on me. Shouldn't drunk that last forty
but lifting scrap all day for a twenty was rough
just needed a little something: sore, dirty

tired, then pigs pull me over a block
from the pad - same old LAPD bull shit,
but I stumble walking the line and they lock
me down, my mother will throw a fit

when the neighbors tell her. Damn, my head hurts.
I can hear all these folks screaming, won't help
nothing, they only beat me worse and worse
Is that my uncle yelling? Why? I felt

all this before. Now they will beat the hell
out of me, but how I get rid of their smell?

Florence & Normandie (April, 1992)

vii
I need to do something. Can't believe what
them boys doing to the white folks that drive
by - its stupid. Them folks didn't beat up
that drunk man, why hurt folks who just drive

down a black street. I'm seventy- two years
old but gotta get from behind this walker
and do something, now they pulling man clear
out his truck like he a hog they going slaughter

this is wrong, wrong; police left, TV people
just watching like they want to show us savage
them three ain't good for nothing but drink, needle
now this, throwing cinder blocks, doing damage

to all of us that's stayed here - it ain't right
over four cops we knew be free - it ain't right.

viii
They got me on tape gunning it in reverse
Damn! Don't believe that - *protect and serve*
logo seems large, but hell, we rehearsed
this - verdict in and we got the good word

they all walked, so now the hood explodes
and we pull out, let them burn their own jungle,
but I'm ghetto deep when we get the code
to get back to station and it all crumbles:

Pico Union, K-Town, South Central, the Valley
craziness because the folks in Simi
know that what happens in an alley
in LA is only about all the seamy

shit they worked hard to leave behind
for tract homes, good schools, and their own kind.

ix
I wouldn't want to be white here today
not after that news out of Simi,
no surprise, them folks think black man splayed
on asphalt is like olives in martini-

just custom; should have taken another
way to pick up my kids, what is this traffic?
All those copters circling almost smother
other sounds, can't figure out the racket

up ahead even with AC off and window down,
should have just stayed on the damn freeway,
but CHP closing off ramps to downtown
before they riot gear up, to keep away

any madness from the money, except skid
row, how the hell I'm gonna get my kids.

103rd Street (August, 1965)

x
We finally got bayonets and bullets
this morning. All it took was three of us
hurt; driver didn't even pretend to pull up
to roadblock, just floored it and crushed

those soldiers. Now we got two shots a piece
if it comes to that. Lots of pissed off folks
here about way more than how those cops beat
up that boy. These slums are no fucking joke

look better than back east, not stacked up
against each other, but you can smell poor-
Harlem, Chicago may look a lot more tough
but behind this stucco and sliding glass doors

is pure ghetto: full of fury and fear
that grows when I give this jeep a slow steer.

xi
Why, why are we burning our own block?
I know the church, rectory will be okay,
but where folks going to buy milk? Those rocks
broke more than windows, white folks feel betrayed-

they ran those stores for over a decade
all the hard liquor, beer, wine there hurt
but bread, eggs on shelf, even if you paid
too much, now flames in front a tank turret.

What do I say from the pulpit about all this?
What scripture will rinse away all this rage?
No supermarkets here, even with raised fists
no jobs but selling drugs, flesh on streets made

harder by lack of anything but poor
so nothing here now but slam of a screen door.

xii
They prone me out again like a beat dog
right in front of my mama's cactus bed
like I ain't nothing, like the stink and fog-
tear gas, white boy aftershave makes me dead,

too dead to do a damn thing about this shit
but they going have to kill my ass for real
now if they think they can roll up and spit
on this hood; even in tanks they can't steal

respect from these streets. Watts take everything
every damn thing if you ain't ready
to go all the way down. These soldiers see a ring
of fire soon, cause they don't know steady

in the face of I just don't care about the hurt
if I can bloody up that new camouflage shirt.

30708

246

MAY 11 1938

Interviewer   Samuel S. Taylor
Person interviewed   Ellen Brass
                   1427 W. Eighth Street, Little Rock, Arkansas
Age   About 82

---------- [White Folks Want Niggers]

"I was born in Alabama in Green County. I was about four years old when I came from there; so I don't know much about it. I growed up in Catahoula, Louisiana. My mother's name was Caroline Butler and my father's name was Lee Butler. One of my father's brothers was named Sam Butler. I used to be a Butler myself, but I married. My father and mother were both slaves. They never did any slave work.

Father Free Raised

"My father was free raised. The white folks raised him. I don't know how he became free. All that I know is that he was raised right in the house with the white folks and was free. His mother and father were both slaves. I was quite small at the time and didn't know much. They bought us like cattle and carried us from place to place.

Slave Houses

"The slaves lived in log cabins with one room. I don't know what kind of house the white folks lived in. They, the colored folks, ate corn bread, wheat bread (they raised wheat in those times), pickled pork. They made the flour right on the plantation. George Harris, a white man, was the one who brought me out of Louisiana into this State. We traveled in wagons in those days. George Harris owned us in Louisiana.

Slave Sales

"We were sold from George Harris to Ben Hickinbottom. They bought us then like cattle. I don't know whether it was a auction sale or a private sale. I am telling it as near as I know it, and I am telling the truth. Hickinbottom brought us to Catahoula Parish in Louisiana. Did I say Harris brought us? Well, Hickinbottom brought us to Louisiana. I don't know why they went from one place to the other like that. The soldiers were bad about freeing the slaves. From Catahoula Parish, Hickinbottom carried us to Alexandria, Louisiana, and in Alexandria, we was set free.

How Freedom Came

"According to my remembrance the Yankees come around and told the people they was free. I was in Alexandria, Louisiana. They told the colored folks they was free and to go and take what they wanted from the white folks. They had us all out in the yard dancing and playing. They sang the song:

> 'They hung Jeff Davis on a sour apple tree
> While we all go marching on.'

It wasn't the white folks on the plantation that told us we was free. It was the soldiers their selves that came around and told us. We called 'em Yankees.

Right After the War

"Right after the War, my folks farmed--raised cotton and corn. My mother had died before I left Alabama. They claimed I was four years old when my mother died in Alabama. My father died after freedom.

Occupation

"My first occupation was farming--you know, field work. Sometimes I used to work around the white people too--clean house and like that.

Random Opinions

"The white folks ain't got no reason to mistreat the colored people. They need us all the time. They don't want no food unless a nigger cooks it. They want niggers to do all their washing and ironing. They want niggers to do their sweeping and cleaning and everything around their houses. The niggers handle everything they wears and hands them everything they eat and drink. Ain't nobody can get closer to a white person than a colored person. If we'd a wanted to kill 'em, they'd a all done been dead. They ain't no reason for white people mistreating colored people."

Walk on a New England Beach After the Mansion Tour

A gull sits on a log nestled in brackish ice etched with salt streaks surrounded by hurricane lumber. *Mother, I am sorry there is nothing to say on this birthday of my dead brother.* We walk gingerly on the battered boardwalk around branches stumps of oak, maple, ash, taken by the sea then spit back where sand had been.

"Both of my granddaughters have an affinity for Latin men."

"Mother, how am I supposed to respond to that?"

"I am ninety, you don't respond, you just listen.
You know son, when the tour guide said shipping, he meant slaves."

Frozen cattails jut out the edges of the only dune left.

"You should have said something son, this is your home now, raised your hand, told him, "Look closely at that ship in the bottle on the bookcase young man, look at all the iron, despite all the barrels on deck, rum was never the point."

Back Brace

Thirty inch piece of hickory, honed smooth
round and straight until it eases into a bone handle
sweat creviced by fingers and a thumb.
This stick has buttressed bad legs, busted backs
for generations: great grandfather, grandfather, father,
and now it is not a decoration anymore.
Not just propped in the corner, leaned gracefully
between Bearden print and the table with clothes hanger
sculptures made on Central Boulevard by old Mr. Darnell:
bending wire into ghetto filigree so fine you hear the sax
playing from solder and metal, you taste the forehead
salt from the hatted figure bent over a wire plow.

The handle hardens when fingers grip, then you lean
onto it, providing a different weight to the legacy,
stiffening quick what's left of spine; shielding a leg
that won't always work anymore, each step
dragging into fresh ground that is harder,
more unforgiving than the drought baked adobe
you took your first steps on. The worn out discs,
the arthritic vertebrate force sharp decisions about
the commonplace; stairs instead of slow elevator,
step count desire for second coffee. What do I take today,
the thin three book backpack with pencil, yellow
pad, or journal in fat briefcase ripe with raw poems?

ii

Nobody would have dared told grand pop
he had to cot rest each afternoon, that his Arkansas
morning had to start with a steaming
towel on spine instead of boots and a shovel
misting up quick with shit after cleaning the mule stall
and slopping half-feral pigs penned at far
edge of the old pasture in the middle of saplings
rubbed crooked in grass beat down to the roots.
Grand pop always pointed proudly to the brace
on his back, tied in knots of wood and leather, telling
all of us young ones his daddy worked a hundred
plus acres for days with a hurt back and no help,

nothing like this. Grand pop got it from Doc Johnson
after his first bad fall, using it let him back
behind the plow in less than a week, better off
than his father - that old man would moan himself
into most mornings, just straightening himself
enough each day to build a life fresh from shackles
busting dirt into rows of tomatoes, okra, collards and corn,
sweet and feed, to roast straight over the fire or fatten up
hogs that spent most of their short life in the forest,
while he ran a few scrawny cattle that grew
into a herd to make all of our worlds about more
than cotton and sacks that paid less each season.

iii

Pop told us all this with a smile, all of it
when my brothers and I asked about the ruler
straight keloids on his back. He told us those bumps
covered a metal rod fused into bone
at the VA hospital. He didn't tell us it was
payment for learning enough Korean to ask directions,
recognizing the smell of kimchee or ability
to work numbers with pencil and pad
to drop an explosive into space the size
of a closet, queen bed, sandbox from miles away
before packing that big gun back on a flatbed
to obey the crackling on the two-way to the next spot.

He did tell us his crew never saw a body
they had anything to do with, no chunks of blasted
flesh, no smeared blood, no charred piles
of bones scattered among fox holes, village huts,
river banks with flat rocks perfect for laundry,
marking a signpost for that moment
the thunder turned man made and the rain
became metal that sieved and separated flesh.
But one day he told us, loading ammo boxes on that
truck, the back popped, the left leg tightened
from hamstring to knee and he could smell mule
rising clear from the dark mud in that rice paddy.

iv

I don't ever remember his grimace,
the jaw tightening into a twisted face
that mirrors each of my mornings. I don't remember
one single groan when he stood up, reached
down to tie his shoe, walked us to school
or hit ground ball after ball to us in the backyard
to make sure we would watch it all the way
into the glove. I don't ever remember him hesitating
behind a wheelbarrow loaded with cinder blocks
or pausing before hoisting two twenty-five pound
sacks of concrete on his shoulders to build
a fence around all of our lives.

There's no image in my head of Pop bent over
grasping for breath in a swirl of pain and madness
knowing the numbness will arch hard
down spine, land in hip, then shoot into left
knee before freezing the calf and making the Achilles
ache with a sharp stab each time you take a step
so hurt and helplessness mesh with
real respect for phrase you have made into
metaphor, a casual joke with fake punch line
that you are an old black man that just wants
to sit in peace after fishing with ice tea, collards laced
with vinegar, pepper, and small bits of ham.

v

Grandfather wouldn't leave that Arkansas dirt.
He worked that truck garden until he was eighty-five
and only stopped after they pulled him out
out of there; after a week of unanswered calls
found in bed, twenty pounds thin, freezer full of fish
dressed out doe hanging in the cold room.
He barely recognized his two oldest, as they marveled
at rows of tomatoes, collards, okra and corn
busting up through red clay tamed by chicken shit
and fish cleanings that forced dirt to cradle
seed in rows worked for his table or maybe trade
not some doughy soft hand with a smudged ledger

and fingers clinching half the dollars that sack
was worth with a pale smile and knowledge that load
would sell easy for triple the next day.
That old man pulled on wood and leather
tied together each morning, lacing the stays
in the front while sucking in his breath
until the curved board in back snugged tight
against his spine, doing what his body no longer
could, melding muscle, bone into one thing
that could handle a team of mules, shovel manure
pull rocks and stumps out the way of that plow
blade on the last ten acres he worked.

vi

First, a dull throb in the lower back, then a small
sear of pain from waist to hip widening just below
knee that spreads to calf then ankle before
it all goes numb, leaving no choice but to have
each finger grasp knuckle hard the handrail
to keep as Auntie would say "from calling the wrong
kind of attention to yourself." All you can do
is pray for continued emptiness of the stairwell,
and the damn thing to come back: hope for slight tingle
like a wire brush barely grazing the skin, than needle
points followed by cramping then hurt washing over
spine until it all jerks back to your own desire.

The hamstring, then knee, then calf convulse slowly
in a choppy unison just a moment before
muscles mesh slow together once again to move
forward one shaky step after another to office
and padded chair or straight to truck where you
must consider the big step into the driver seat
and the odds the leg will work accelerator, brake pedal
enough to straight shot 32 safe to home
where you can calculate the pain in pulling a rake
or pushing a wheelbarrow out to raised beds
with stubborn tomatoes that won't grace a New England
June surrounded by red okra that will not flower.

vii

The bone handle is worn into a "T," hollowed
comfortable underneath for each finger,
discolored pretty with sweat marks from three
generations ice smooth for palm flesh
to set firm and easy, buttressing bum leg
and a busted back, which is most of what we know
about the old man who made this—
grandfather, father only had the sparest stories
to fill in rocks, dirt and fallow fields we walked
on each summer, culling firewood from forests that
hadn't been touched for half a generation and fishing
creeks that had never seen a hook bounce

off the gravel bottoms or get hung in honeysuckle
along the banks. Grandfather, father never
talked much about the rolling pins, spoons, chair, table
he carved still used everyday, even walking
across the crumbling stone foundations for that row
of cabins on the other side of the land where
he built the home place, nobody explained
how he did this, why he kept the name of his last owner
while cutting hand hewn beams, forging square nails
before using a hand plane to smooth wide planks of hickory
that shrank tight for our generation that walked
on something besides carpet for the very first time.

viii

Nobody knows if Great Grandfather had that busted back
when he walked off the slave farm in Georgia
and liked the feel and taste of the dirt in Arkansas,
nobody remembers the very first time
they saw him grimace or heard him moan
almost silent bending over a fresh shot rabbit
or dressing out a deer, harnessing a team
or working hard a row of sweet potatoes, pulling
thirty, forty pounds into a sack with ease.
Grandfather and the great aunts always talked
about how the old man carved things, about how
they remember when that cane was finished

long before he really needed it: choice piece
of hickory, hand etched bone handle, set careful
in the corner after being rubbed smooth with lard.
That stick went years without use, just sat there as one
more thing he cut out wood to use in his life
until he fell off half-broken horse or was kicked hard
in the middle of the back by a mule after a day of plowing:
my great aunts and uncle would argue on Sundays
after supper during homecoming over which story
was right, they would squabble over dominos, watermelon
and hard cider, never disagreeing you could hear
clear each morning clicks and pops in his spine.

ix

Grand Pop just let that cane sit for years
with the few other wooden plates, bowls, Bible
in the corner shelf holding what little
was left from before the surrender. Later,
he just let the cane sit next to the door
as he strapped up slow and careful each morning.
First, easing arms and shoulders into leather
straps then cinching belt around waist before he buckled
one by one each of the three straps across his chest
and stomach until leather bit flesh, until that curved
piece of wood riding his backbone would clasp
on deep enough to leave narrow grooves in the skin

that looked like whip marks or furrows on a fresh
plowed field. Then he would grab tight
the bottom on each side of his waist and tug down
hard three times to take out the gaps and creases
as he walked out the door to meet no one at his barn
but the day's work he wanted to do.
The leather straps darkened deeper than his copper
colored skin, the piece of carved oak that shaped
his spine gained a slow gloss shadowing the grain.
At first light he would start, stiff and slow,
but limber up steady bit by bit so that by noon
he could shovel with just a small grimace.

x

Pop used to soak in the tub with the steam rising
in clouds because the water was so hot
it would almost scald your fingers, right after
hauling that leather sack of letters
up and down those hills in Boyle Heights before
classes at night school or at the second job.
After soaking for a hard five minutes
he would bend each knee to chest as slow as possible
to loosen the twisted knot around his spine.
The first operation left a long razor straight scar
to the left of the spine from shoulder blade to his waist
the skin mottling up into ridges and valleys

like lava fresh frozen across a field of chocolate brown
that shimmered with sweat as he lifted two twenty-five
pound sacks of concrete in our new backyard
to smooth LA adobe into a patio and path to collard
green, okra and tomato garden framed by gladiolas
and bougainvillea blooming most of the spring and summer.
But even lifting those sacks or raking out the clumps
in that clay it was always the roses he marveled at;
once bent over the hose for a long drink in eighty-five
degrees between sacks in December, he pointed
at my mother's garden, and a rose opened in deep silver
never saying a word, but stopping for a minute,
put the sack on his shoulder, looked at me and smiled.

xi

The new pull of metal against bone hesitates
the hips, halts the half-bend in the waist,
while both biceps tense up with the weight
of a full shovel of snow off the woodpile.
Twenty degrees makes the rods shimmy
against vertebrate each time you twist
to sweep another layer off the stiff tarp,
tightening the strips of composite holding
in the discs so that after all these years
you finally don't feel broken anymore.
Your limit should be three logs split in half
in one load, but limits lay harder

and harder each year so bending the knees
is deliberate consolation for swinging that strap
over shoulder holding a thick half frozen five
pieces that still feels miraculous
without sear of hurt lancing gut to groin,
calling out the times beer gutted hauling cinder blocks
sacks of concrete on shoulders for a wage
that would barely cover the necessary sins,
until now when that cane goes back on the wall
between that Bearden print and wire figurines
to wait for the creak, the sear, the sharp echo
in barn door, in mule bray, in whatever's next.

Suet

After Phillip Seymour Hoffman

My boxers worry and whine about the cardinals fighting
with finches in the snow under the feeder in front of
the big bay window. They yelp, growl, then retreat
to the rug and wood stove blazing aspen and red oak.
Another birthday, and there is no dance of aging bones
on the sand this year because Hermosa Beach is 3000
miles away, and both drummers are half a decade dead.
GW and Tommy P. could coax coffee cans and plastic buckets
to melody with bent spoons and dinged-up butter knives
beating out a sweet sweat rhythm on seaweed and sand.

This is a brutal season, offering up only the blunt gift
of bone-drenching heat from a fire that must be tended
in a life that must be tended: right hand flat against the bar,
or against the table, or against the one-year older thigh
because one finger in the air calls more than an odd shaped
chilled glass containing two shots of the best gin
anchored securely by three vermouth swollen olives.
That hand, that one finger in the air, could summon the rage
spoon-heated into thirty years of empty syringes
heaped inside a closet in Compton waiting to be claimed.

I finally understand all the debris piles up in unlit places
without stink. It does not matter if the track marks
are scabbed over and scarred clean. It does not matter
if the ancient keloid running down your gut from a blade
you barely remember is almost smooth now between
stretch marks and loose skin. It does not matter
if you finally understand that some birds overwinter,
there is still that insistent itch up and down old scars
that those red feathers should be far south, instead of breaching
this raw whiteness oozing all the slow grief in beauty.

After Church

My father always listened to you Sundays
the only time he would sit hard on the couch
paper in hand while your voice wrapped

around a week of mail delivery, night school
hitting us ground balls on groomed grass
shaved careful by an ancient push mower

that first he coaxed, cajoled, then just told
one of us to use each Saturday because "why buy
a power mower when I have three of them."

Your voice Lena stitched tight into that big band
to make a quilt covering hours between
service and Sunday dinner on creaky picnic table

weighed down with smothered pork chops
black-eyed peas and dirty rice making chicken
livers sweet in the early Compton evening

smelling of ripe peaches and night jasmine
me and my brothers holding full paper plates
with your voice serving as an amen.

Let The Good Times

You smiled about that five dollars a day
to clean house for rich folks - instead of two
nickels a row for a sack that never weighed
enough to bargain away all those blues
from fields that made this a second city
to no place, because turnip greens, hot water
cornbread, calluses and eternity
preached over rows fertilized with slaughter
grew that Mississippi harmony
into a howl that halted the chatter
humid with cigars and liquor for a cotton colony
that shakes off the cold for what happens after:
stiff shoes and flush toilets that sweetens bass, drum
to smell that dirt again through smoke and rum.

Good Deal

Half-splash from the June creek graces the ravine
with stale truth that everything aches now
fingers, ankles, knees: throbbing mean
to muffled drum echoing off a rusted plow
that chalk out the limits to this life,
sifting damp ash for paper, colored stone
old coin with a busted screen torn and rife
with lies still not sorted from splintered bone.
I would make that Robert Johnson deal
now, decades for sugar tit of one line
to arch blood, pus and vowels over the real
chasm between the old stories and mine,
because no demon can do this kind of harm;
each word each line nuzzling silence in my arms.

30776

MAY 21 1938

Interviewer　　　　　　　　Samuel S. Taylor
Person interviewed　　　　Silas Dothrum
　　　　　　　　1419 Pulaski Street, Little Rock, Arkansas
Age　82 or 83　　　　Occupation Field hand, general work

[Don't Know Nothin']

"The white people that owned me are all dead. I am in this world by myself. Do you know anything that a man can put on his leg to keep the flies off it when it has sores on it? I had the city doctor here, but he didn't do me no good. I have to tie these rags around my foot to keep the flies off the sores.

"I worked with a white man nineteen years—put all that concrete down out there. He is still living. He helps me a little sometimes. If it weren't for him I couldn't live. The government allows me and my wife together eight dollars a month. I asked for more, but I couldn't get it. I get commodities too. They amount to about a dollar and a half a month. They don't give any flour or meat. Last month they gave some eggs and those were nice. What they give is a help to a man in my condition.

"I don't know where I was born and I don't know when. I know I am eighty-two or eighty-three years old. The white folks that raised me told me how old I was. I never saw my father and my mother in my life. I don't know nothin'. I'm just an old green man. I don't know none of my kin people—father, mother, uncles, cousins, nothin'. When I found myself the white people had me.

"That was right down here in Arkansas here on old Dick Fletcher's farm. There was a big family of them Fletchers. They took me to Harriet Lindsay to raise. She is dead. She had a husband and he is dead. She had two or three daughters and they are dead.

Slave Houses

"I can remember what they used to live in. The slaves lived in old wooden houses. They ain't living in no houses now—one-half of them. They were log houses—two rooms. I have forgot what kind of floors—dirt, I guess. Food was kept in a smokehouse.

Relatives

"The whole family of Fletchers is dead. I think that there is a Jef Fletcher living in this town. I don't know just where but I met him sometime ago. He doesn't do nothing for me. Nobody gives me anything for myself but the man I used to work for—the concrete man. He's a man.

How Freedom Came

"All I remember is that they boxed us all up in covered wagons and carried us to Texas and kept us there till freedom came. Then they told us we were free and could go where wanted. But they kept me in bondage and a girl that used to be with them. We were bound to them that we would have to stay with them. They kept me just the same as under bondage. I wasn't allowed no kind of say-so.

"After Dick Fletcher died, his wife and his two children fetched us back—fetched us back in a covered wagon.

"I am a Arkansas man. Was raised here. I am very well known here, too. Some years after that she turned us loose. I can't remember just how many years it was, but it was a good many.

Right After the War

"After Mrs. Fletcher turned us loose, we worked with some families. I was working by the year. If I broke anything they took it out of my wages. If I broke a plow they would charge me for it. I was working for niggers. I can't remember how much they paid, but it wasn't anything when they got through taking out. I'm dogged if I know how much they were supposed to pay; it has been so long. But I know that if I broke anything—a tool or something—they charged me for it. I didn't have much at the end of the year. It would take me a lifetime to make anything if I had to do that.

Patrollers

"I have been out in the bushes when the pateroles would come up and gone into log houses and get niggers and whip their asses. They would surround all the niggers and make them go into the house where they could whip them as much as they wanted to. All that is been years and years ago. I never seen any niggers get away from them. I have heered of them getting away, but if they did I never knowed it.

Ku Klux Klan

"I heered of the Ku Klux, but they never bothered me. I never saw them do anything to anybody.

Recollections Relating to Parents

"I don't know who my parents were, but it seems like I heard them say my father was a white man, and I seem to remember that they said my mother was a dark woman.

4.

Opinions

"The young people today ain't worth a shit. These young people going to school don't mean good to nobody. They dance all the night and all the time, and do everything else. That man across the street runs a whiskey house where they dance and do everything they're big enough to do. They ain't worth nothing."

Middle Aged in Montego Bay

Not the noise, not all the blackness, not the smell
that greets you from you: wounded, reeking hard
of fear and freedom from a world charred
by loss to the rhythm of a brisk death knell
that here, just might reggae down to expel
all the careful demons stalking mid-life
in this sweaty taxi on brand new blacktop tight
against a turquoise sea shadowed by chards
that could be fish, forgotten wrecks, coral
or just the sun falling away from this rock
seeded by blood and bones which quarrel
with the small surrenders each day that mock
your ancestors, mock your awe at these three girls:
head baskets, braids, dancing into a dark whirl.

Camouflage

Our safe, sound Connecticut kids don't know Soweto
or even a Watts dark enough to dance
ghetto fabulous to Sly Stone for the slow
purge of desire only Oakland Funk can lance
out a father that sometimes still dreams needle:
even with leather sofa, big screen, ottoman
camouflaging scars which can't wheedle
a tear, a twenty, a tired scowl from woman
who still listens to our children like a liturgy
without incense, organ, hymns or silence
after murmured amen to buttress liberty
a raised ranch provides against the violence
of life with no pool, no lawn that is a spectacular green
when shadow of projects flare with a sudden sheen.

Clean

The flowered bathrobe with Micky Mouse house slippers
the creaky wheel on the IV up and down
the hall every two hours before she screams at
the nurses for more Oxy, flashing splotchy skin
    wrinkled hip at least a decade older than
the spine you just got rebuilt; a spine seven years older than
the last time one of those blue, pink tablets
    carefully caressed the tongue and slide down
the throat propelled by Tanqueray, Jack Daniels, or
the best Zinfandel or Cabernet available.
    So now you don't have a choice to lovingly thumb

the morphine button because it is not there, just
the nurse with a Dixie cup, two Tylenol, and a smile at
the *courage you have*, because *how can you do this*
the spine being *just a bundle of nerves and all*
    while the twenty-year old boy in
the bed on the other side of the curtain moans until
the top of each hour and his Demerol drip arrives to boost
    his Fentanyl pills because whimpering hard when
the doctors do rounds about seventy five screws in hips, and
the six pins in his neck works, because *they must understand
    it really, really hurts* and *why did they take away*

the Vicodin pills - extended release - because
the pain is *very, very bad* and everything is gone;
the crashed Harley from mother, the job at the nightclub
the girl who has only visited twice and refused to do him
    in his hospital bed when the staff was busy. And now,
the nurses won't wipe his butt, they say he must use
the plastic bedpan even through it hurts, and point
    to that old black guy *not using anything* except a chant
that pain is only weakness leaving the body, but I know now
the mantra is a lie, the pain never goes anywhere
    it is an accumulation of all our losses, like

the blood in what looks like a tobacco tin at the end of
the tube draining wound left by surgeon to make

the new spine, the tube that keeps getting blocked, that
the physician's assistant tells me each time she pinches it clear
    you can't go home until it stops flowing because
the skin will sprout a hematoma instead of a scar between
the titanium and nerves that now glide unencumbered
    by jagged bone that lanced with every bend toward
the bad feet, stabbed with every twist for decades until
the scalpel sliced into a past you cannot forget and
    now must clot to avoid surrender to the last false thing.

III

I was sold out of Russell County during the war. Ol' Man Menefee refugeed me into Tennessee near Knoxville. They sold me down there to a man named Jim Madden. He carried me down in Virginny near Lynchburg and sold me to Jim Alec Wright. He was the man I was with at the time of the surrender. Then I was in a town called Liberty.

Henry Banner
County Hospital
Little Rock, Ark

No Shotgun

I. Fourteen

With no shotgun involved there was a chance
the box: walnut, oak, pine, could be open,
because even after three bullets lance
a heart that will never be broken
you can still have that lid cracked.
Do the whole history thing, be put away
like grandpa and his grandpa: tracts stacked
next to a photo, the guest book and brutal cliché

of stomach sobs for another black boy.
Nurses flank aisles, pressed hair, starch whites
circling old ones because grief is no ploy
after eighty, lit up by shards of light
arching through colored glass of that last meal
so folks can whisper: he looks real, so very real.

II. Fifty-Four

Right after realizing all the screaming
waking me was me--did I feel the staples:
grasp for switch and sweet opiate dreaming
to smooth sutured belly and brittle fable
that is old age, because grief is not a surprise
anymore. Loss after loss welts this body
that refuses to see how scars disguise
a goodbye ripe with all the shoddy

rituals that suffer an old black man.
High blood pressure, bad kidneys, vinegar gut
that robs pleasure from collards and ham.
None of you did this. Wave off wheelchair and strut
into grey hair, bad joints, sagging muscles
that laugh each morning at this one last hustle.

Sledgehammer Goodbye

Eugene, 1971

The squat square crunches the tinted glass. First
blow sprays slivers back to where the hickory
handle meets metal. Second blow causes it to bow
toward the steering wheel still dappled
with blood and tiny chunks of chocolate colored
flesh and small naps of hair. The third blow
chasms the windshield onto the mocha leather dash
he had picked through a cargo bin at the tannery
for hours to find: streaked now, with dark splatters.
Fingers tighten into splinters as muscles tense
for another swing, brushing police tape before
arcing up, then hurtling down into glass that peppers
everything: skull shift knob, sheepskin seat covers,
leather headliner. "This piece of shit killed him,
not none of you weak bastards wearing red."
Six pounds of bolt metal moves deliberate
into primer, two coats of paint and clear
that blew them away on Avalon Boulevard
first time he rolled up to Fat Burger,
circling the whole lot slow and easy before
backing into one of the prime spaces to the left
of the pick up window. That paint pockmarked
from a nine millimeter and sawed off
still shimmers a tense blue hard in this hood,
damp from the first night ever outside
since new life was breathed into this 63,
new chrome, new paint, each nut, each bolt.
The rhythm in the swing starts to step up,
got to be gone before cops, wanna- bees
see him violating this crime scene,
because he hadn't rolled with him last night
and now there was a filled slab, a busted body
and bastards he'd have to hunt.
Curtains begin cracking up and down the block
because even this early between trash truck,
street sweeper, the steady smash of metal, glass
sounds odd, less familiar, than sixteen

shots, ten shotgun blasts into a cherry impala,
and a 17 year old with a flat tire on a Friday night.

Junkyard Lace

Mr. Vernell, 1971

I hate they burying that boy tomorrow,
nobody should be put in the ground
on a damn Wednesday, it's a day for lunch
specials, start to look for the check from the VA
not crawling into a tight mourning suit.
Francine came by, says his momma wants
the box open, she wanted to collect
what she could, it's going to cost so damn
much to fix his face. I watched him walk
to school since he was out in the world,
all them boys loved my junk yard
but him, he mostly loved that one ride-
boy noticed it the day it was towed in,
stared at it a week before he had guts enough
to come up to me and ask, "is the frame
straight?" Now where the hell a fifteen
year old learn to ask something smart
like that. I saw more of the shit them kids
went through than I wanted, sitting here
in my fenced-in block of rust and metal.
Saw them run from them hoods wearing red,
saw the police beat them for nothing, saw
them circle up with a joint for the first time
over in that parking lot; could tell because
the coughing damn near bent each of them
to the blacktop. After that boy walked
by that 63 for eight months looking at it
like something in black lace, no surprise
when he shuffled up with a little wad
of twenties so nervous he could barely
mouth "how much?" I told him to keep his roll,
just get it off my yard by end of the week.
Then he made it a rare thing- metal work
engine rebuild—a rare thing, he read up, took
shop, scrounged this yard so damn hard for parts
had to hire him, he knew more than me where
shit was and now he on a slab: better

he be in Nam with Chinese cats trying to off him
than to end up like this. Now there ain't
nothing, nothing but a mamma learning
blood tears, black boys getting ready to hunt
black boys, and a sweet ass wreck ice picked
with buckshot and hollow points being
towed into some white man's junkyard.

Undertaker's Aria

Mrs. Ardel Johnson, 1971

The big yellow sponge glides from ankle
to dull pink crater laced by purple veins
where the knee should be: a small canyon
circled by a chocolate rim of skin
that foams disinfectant blue when liquid
seeps in the dots of buckshot, dimpling
wound and penny holes spread across thighs,
stomach and chest. Then the soft bristle brush
scours gentle each mound raised around lead
lanced flesh. The dry towel follows-
working down the legs and torso to dislodge flecks
of blood, chunks of skin, stray hairs, chemical
stains from autopsy. The blue-tinged crimson
liquid doesn't pool in the coffin size sink
under neck, below armpits, between legs
because long thin beige fingers clear drain
before grasping the butter knife to press
putty into each of the sixteen holes.
A pointed plastic tube slides in artery
by collar bone and blood sputters out,
slow at first, then faster when the second tube
slips in thigh vein to pump formaldehyde
steady into the slow stiffening flesh.
Butter knife enters mouth and pushes left
side of the face back to where it belongs,
no picture necessary because she understands
the curve of the jaw, angle of the chin and pads
cheek with plaster before sealing the lips.
Corn rolls make the hair easy, holes on back
of the head are hidden by pillow, so she just needs
to buff the scalp then oil to make the braids
glisten. "Cousin Francine was worried about his
face, but those three holes in his neck, one
in the temple will be the challenge. They going
to take another day. But Mr Vernell
sent a check so I can get extra help
for all my other work, and make this boy
look just like himself for his mama."

Salt and Fear

Miss Francine Johnson, 1971

Don't know what to tell her about his face,
Ardel will act matter of fact if I call,
but Gail is his mamma, and coming back
from the morgue that's all she talked about:
how them animals ruined her baby's
face. I reminded her the Johnsons been putting
black folks in the ground real nice since
the surrender, since Great Grandpa Ryan
left Savannah for home place in Arkansas,
since the forty years the whole church picked up
and came to Compton. Although 'till riots
five summers back we just told folks back home
we were in LA. No need now, everybody
knows Compton, it was all over the TV,
like Saigon, like Johannesburg, they all
know where we are. But I don't know what
to say to Gail. I'm going over with
a covered dish later, and she will ask.
My faith's in cousin Ardel, she's fixed
faces from bullet holes for five years now,
black boys shooting each other over blocks
of alleys, liquor stores and churches.
Gail's going to ask - then fold in half
and start to wail. I hate that sound wherever
it happens, waiting room at Saint Jude's,
mortuary chapel, the path between the rose garden
and graves at Green Hills, I hate that sound.
The pitch is difficult on the ears,
mamas burying their boys always seem
to raise up that same slow acid note
that feels like cactus and burning asphalt.
It's what I like least about this work.
The rest is all right, you can soften suffering:
help them pick a box they can pay for
get them to settle on a service,
picture for the pamphlet, flowers, music
that fit a grief-only budget. But that wail

weighs all that beauty down onto wax flesh
setting on satin. The pastor's sermon,
the sweet hymns, the tired words, whispers
from congregation sink into that open
box, covered by a woman issuing
a terrible sound, as she strains through salt
and fear to see if they fixed her boy's face.

Leather

Barbara Jean Simmons, 1971

Eight bullet holes in driver-side front
panel, nine millimeter. Two shotgun
blasts on left tire, buckshot patterns on
metal rims indicate close range. Wheel
slightly pancaked, victim drove with a flat
tire for some distance (why was he trying
to drive back to freeway? No matter,
need to process this scene, file the report).
Seventeen holes in door, same caliber,
widespread dimpling on paint indicates
multiple shotgun blasts into same door.
Window, not enough intact glass to determine
precise number. (I'm glad the coroner
was quick, want to finish up, be out of here
by dark, three patrol cars covering
is not enough). Blood splatter on dashboard,
seats, show victim struck by buckshot
at close range. Fourteen holes in trunk,
back window, different caliber, forty-five
or larger. Pattern framed by intact glass
shows shots were discharged from medium
distance, mostly into empty passenger
seat. Holes in left-side center console,
inside panel indicate door was opened
during assault, substantial chunks of flesh
mixed with blood spray reflect direct
hit on extremity. (That leather
is gorgeous, even stained it shimmers.
Would make a great coat or purse).
Tuffs of hair, matter on seat indicate
victim was prone while shots were fired,
head and neck protected by half closed door
accounting for large volume of wounds
to chest and torso area: this is confirmed
by large volume of blood on asphalt.
Pocking in blacktop around door area
indicates significant weapons discharge
took place after subject was laying in street.

Double Fat and Fries

Jerome Abernathy Lewis, 1971

I knew they would leave his space open,
he'd always park just left of the pick up
window, so you'd get a long look at that ride
when you get that double fat and fries.
They all had to all roll into Fat Burger
after this funeral, had to—been managing
this joint four years and ain't never going
to be nothing like today. Sweetest rides
in the hood will be bouncing this blacktop
till curfew, don't think police will come on
they own and I ain't calling, not about this
hell no, not about this. He was decent, sure
he ran hard sometimes, liquor, some weed
but he never banged into nothing, no colors
no gang tats, they just offed him because
of where he lived. Some barbaric shit,
and now Eugene and them hunting them hard,
because you just can't let that shit go
you just can't. I got to get out - if they can
put him in the ground, it don't matter how
you walk this life, look at this crowd: car clubs,
jocks, shop rats. He was decent people.
Never took shit, but never gave none neither
a year into trade tech and he's on a slab
because of a bad tire. I finish JC this June,
then I'm gone. Part of me don't want to go -
leaving moms, cousins, homeboys, what I know
but I'm tired of giving it up to these streets
every damn day, calculating risk in
stop for milk, eggs, six pack. Having my head
on a damn swivel when I step on the front
porch to get some air, every car cruising by
every tinted window gliding down
tenses muscle, stiffens bone to deal
with madness infecting these 200 blocks
that used to be a refuge to all the old folks
running from the fields, but now even they say
this asphalt reeks of burnt rope and charred flesh.

Pork Fat and Sorrow

Joyce Walker, 1971

Seventy five pamphlets here tonight
two hundred twenty five left for tomorrow.
Hopefully, there won't be many people
for this viewing, he's going to be buried
open casket in less then twenty-four hours.
How much can you get out of staring at
a dead person. I checked everything.
Ten dozen roses, split between white, yellow.
Dusted that top of the line mahogany box
with the silk satin lining; fifty candles
on both sides does throw a softer
light on him. Somebody spent hours fixing
his face. Still don't look like him, but his Fro
looks better than he ever had it at school,
clean, blown out nice, right amount of Sheen.
The Johnson's billing big time for this,
and I'm here on Friday night for three dollars
an hour. Everybody been putting it in the plate
to bury this boy, but it all ends up
in mostly one pocket. I stacked a hundred
of those little custom bibles, New Testament
only, with his name and twenty-third psalm
on the back. Those will go tonight, some people
will take more than one. I should sweep and dust
one more time before it starts. Francine will
get here and run her white-gloved finger
over everything, working for the Johnson's
isn't that much better than serving white folks.
I want to make it to Fat Burger
tomorrow night, cleaning up at the church,
social hall shouldn't be on me. The food will
be good; his mama is in the choir and them ladies
will lay out a spread in the Hall after service:
double dipped fried chicken, baked greens and grits,
sweet potato pone and crusty mac and cheese.
They saying old man Verdell is paying for a whole
hog to be done. Best thing about working

black folks funerals is the food. The desserts
will be wonderful, grief always calls out
for pork fat and sugar in the ghetto. I'd better
start lighting candles and getting out the tissues
and folding chairs. That's George bringing
his mama, half the choir is with them, I'd better
get more tissues and turn up the air condition.

Bedpans and a Pretty Box

> Mrs. Althea Tompkins, 1971

They will want to hear *Precious Lord*,
everybody does since Martin was killed
and we all learned it was his favorite. But
I've known that boy's mama twenty years,
she will want to start with *Rock of Ages*.
This young man never acted thug-like,
did not make church except Christmas and
Easter, but that's how all the teenagers
are now. I feel bad for his mama, his grandma
too; they going to bring her straight from the nursing
home for this. During our last prayer visit
she didn't seem to understand much,
but she asked me and the girls to sing,
remembered I ran the choir even
with that hundred two years fogging her days.
That old woman probably sorry she
left Arkansas when things clear: separate
water fountains, had to act your place in public
work your body to bone for nothing
but drugs, killings did not take our young
there, and that old woman would be living
in a house with family, not a motel
made into a hospital with strangers
taking care of her. I feel real bad for Gail,
all those double shifts at Saint Jude cleaning
bed pans, washing sheets to pay for her mama's
room, the boy at Trade Tech, and it all ends
in that pretty box in front of the pulpit.
We are going to miss her soprano today
but some folks can't grieve hard and sing.
Me, when I lost my first boy to the needle
I sang, when they sent my second boy home
in a box under that flag, I sang. This
choir, this church has been my whole world
but watching them wheel in his grandma
makes me want to go home. The air is not thick
enough here and that breeze that everyone

loves at four just makes me shiver and hurt
for the ink black that makes a country night,
each star a scar lancing the Arkansas dark.

No Stooping

Grandma Justina, 1971

I don't recognize my face. I know it's me
They putting me back in my bed, the mirror
is right there, but those eyes aren't mine.
They killed my grandbaby. That's what Gail
came to say, I don't feel like talking, just don't
feel like it. This place, these people. It smells
bad all the time, like a toilet just got scrubbed
like you just cleaned up somebody's vomit.
They are going to take me to say goodbye
to my grandson, I understood that, at least
that. He was really a good boy, not pretend
good like all the others say about their grandkids.
He came every week. Every single week
and sat for a bit, didn't just wave and run off
cause he couldn't take the smell or looking
at my frozen face. I never thought I'd want to see
that red dirt again, never thought I want to
feel the smoothed with pain pine boards
in that glorified slave shack again, but in some
ways it be better than this, better than this.
Gail comes by most days but all the others
not much, not much. I never dreamed I would
last a hundred years, forty in this damn
city. We've lost so much, so much. I used to think
it was okay because I hated that damn dirt
hated that farm, hated the day to day
grimness whenever you left the place, walked
into a world that made you go here or there
without feeling. I never liked picking nothing,
and the moment they moved me here I stopped,
all these folks with they gardens are just silly
you can buy good collards and melon at the store,
no need, no need to stoop in the dirt for it.
But this is hard. Saying goodbye to this boy
is hard, don't make no sense, none. Colored water
fountains made sense, colored schools made sense,
two dollars a day made sense, just white folks

meanness cause they ain't masters no more
but us killing us just don't figure. It just don't.

Blood and Metal Flake Blue

Robert Dewy Thomas, 1971

It was a pain in the ass going back
to the yard for the flatbed. But how the
hell was I supposed to know some knuckle
head would take a sledge to this gorgeous
piece of shit, ruin the rims, bust out all
windows, no damn way I could just hook
that thing up and roll. I'll cruise the blocks
on both sides first to see if anybody stupid
be about. It's still early but there could be
garbage out. I want this tow. Piecing out
this ride going to be sweet, the loot is always
in the parts. White drivers hate theses streets,
leave it mostly to me. Five years since high
school but these still my streets - they
can kill you in a god damn minute, but
they can be worked. Can't see nobody-
I'll drive the block once to be sure, too early
for knuckleheads, and all the good folks at
church. They burying this brother Wednesday
didn't know him but heard he was all right,
sure had a gift for body work and engines
even bullet holed and busted up this
is one sweet piece of metal. This block is just bad:
gang houses both ends, no phone for miles.
Turn the corner into a street full of bangers
drinking forties and blowing jays - they don't
care, they just don' t care. But I'll load this ride,
stick it in the back of the yard and it will be gold
when I'm working the counter. All the side
deals, all the side deals - them old men don't go
into the junk, too good, too big time to walk
the yard so I'll pocket the cash. It seems quiet
I'll hook up, pull this thing on the flatbed, fifteen
minutes I'm in the wind. All the blood sets
you back a bit, even though most is in the street
not on that leather, it still sets you back,
an afternoon starts with a full tank, then ends
with blue flakes in a red puddle on blacktop.

Writing Nightmares

The pavement still bleeds there
each trip back red seeps up though a sidewalk,
raised and broken by tree roots and truck tires,
making it hard for all the old men
doing street Que to roll out metal drums cut in half,
pour in Kingsford and hickory that coal up slow and smokes
sweet while the car washes open,
and metal grates on storefronts rise on a Compton morning.
Walking that cracked pavement
I can't feel flesh shudder under the concrete anymore,
there is no smell from blood and urine on asphalt
except when the wife tires of gently
shaking me at 3 am to stop screams into a New England night
that don't make sense decades after body fluids have dried.

She grips my face, each of her palms
pressed against my cheeks and whispers, "your having
a nightmare, nobody's shooting, nobody's dead."
But she's wrong. They all dead.
Each one rotted into piles of embalmed flesh, bone,
laced with colored velvet and velour chards that lined
those pretty boxes we passed
plates for at church and little league. They all dead.
I have to strain memory for names
but no squint is needed to see each separate face blurred
though my son's face, because he is the age now
I was then. Everything is different
nothing is different. During half beat between dream
tyranny, wife whisper I can smell buckshot, car exhaust.

The stink rises up careful
off the sheets before turkey calls bring me back to the star
splattered dark, oak, and sugar maple woods that aren't refuge,
because that would mean
you're still running, and Rosecrans Avenue taught you
refuge only happens in one breath, in one bead of sweat
in one small soiled gesture
at a time. No screen played those killings over and over

each bullet punctuating black flesh into a parenthetical
(thug, criminal, gang member).
Things none of those eighteen year olds were then, things
my son is not now. Here, my kids don't bob and weave
between red bandannas
fists with gang tats and shiny badges etched LAPD.

On this coast our peace officers
have straight brim hats and ankle boots that walk
on 300 years of burial mounds and old village sites
erased by granite memorials.
After escape from sleep the woodpeckers
rhythm the settled rage I radiate from each narrative
the adult children drag home:
random stop, registration check, other suspects that looked.
Along with my balky hip I share this with those
old men 3000 miles away.
I understand now why they sweat over metal drums,
with hickory to flavor store bought coals to coax
smoke into meat that tastes
the other side of Jim Crow. Pulled pork damps down anger.

A chicken thigh that slides
right off the bone eases hurt from plastic handcuffs.
That smoke lets the third generation since the exodus
understand their grandmother
outside in LA heat growing collards, okra they don't eat.
After six hour flight and slow freeway chaos, my gut
can only take a bite of hot link
and a bowl of grits topped with a small chunk of ham.
When the kinfolk leave me for a minute, and nobody's watching,
I slip a lump of stale brown
sugar from the back of mom's pantry between hot corn,
and smoked pig, and watch it sink slow as the sweet lump
dissolves under pork fat,
into a flat brown puddle that stains the steaming white corn.

Epilogue

Traffic Stop

So what you are telling me, is that when the white lady cop walks up
to her window our daughter rolls it down and says, "how can I help you hon?"
That is what you are telling me. Our daughter. Our daughter.
Our first born. The one we spent two decades plus schooling. What?

I need to calm down. Where were they? Glastonbury. Great. Rich.
Very White. Great. They're okay though. The son was with her.
They're on the way home. Oh, you don't think yelling will be productive.
I should think about what I am going to say to her. Scared? I do admit
I'm scared. What do you mean this is what I wanted? What did I used to say?
"Suburban life means no ghetto strife." I was stupid when I said that.
Yeah, I wanted them out of the hood. No, I don't expect LA street savvy
raising them in Connecticut. But "how can I help you hon?" She doesn't

even talk like that. I know I can't have it both ways. They were stopped
for an hour. Nice. They bought the K9 unit in. Nice. But they're okay.
Why do you keep saying I'm the one who wanted them out of the hood.
I don't remember you wanting the tract home across from the projects.

So she swerved to miss a speed bump and a cop pulls her over? That's
when she asks "how can I help you hon?" Like she's a waitress at a diner.
Like she's going to recite the daily specials. What do you mean that comment
will not be helpful. Helpful? In what universe does the sarcastic greeting
"how can I help you hon" to some scared white lady with a gun get her home
in one piece. That's what I give a damn about. Oh, I am sure she knows
she made a mistake. An hour stopped, yeah. What? I'm not making
this about me or you. Okay, you tell me what I should make this about?

Maybe I will make it about the black face frat party at her college last October,
or noose on the dorm door of her friend at college in New Haven, or maybe
I just bring the full size mirror from the hallway, and ask her nicely to point out
where she sees the privilege shared by all those white kids at her small selective
liberal arts college?

The kids she despises because they act so entitled. Oh you don't think
that would be helpful. Hell yes I'm scared! You see the news.
You want me to recite names. She knows the names. You want truth.
The God honest truth. I don't know what to say any damn more.

Preaching be deferential, just get your ass home, not behind bars, on a slab don't seem to be doing a damn thing for the body count. How the hell do you settle into old age when your kids' deal on the streets is a betrayal. When after everything their day-to day marks all of our failures.

Maybe I just que, don't say nothing, just hug em when they walk in and que make some greens, the girl likes collards as much as I do, maybe between ri and cornbread that faint rattle of chains, and dull thud of the short hoe getti louder each day won't smother us all in a slow crescendo of necessary ange

Acknowledgements

The most important acknowledgment in the creation of this book are the individuals who answered questions from strangers representing a government agency about their enslavement with bravery and dignity. I recognize that there is no way I can understand the emotional freight and material risk this act of expression must have had for them, many which were on, or seeking, some type government assistance, while living in an apartheid society. After studying hundreds of these transcriptions from a historical place of privilege I recognize the powerful gift these narratives provide of a tangible, material connection to my own past. These words reinforce my gratitude for the fortitude of relatives from that generation whose stories fired my imagination and carved out my aesthetic. The authenticity of the responses of these formerly enslaved men and women, which in the majority of cases happened in the context of a racist tone and condescending demeanor from the reviewer, helped me understand the power of voice. Perhaps most importantly, I felt they provided a connection to Conway, Arkansas; a place as a young black man growing up in Los Angeles I knew only as a summer retreat from time on my grandfather's farm. Like many of my peers born a generation after the great migration that spread Black life to cities in the West and North, the south meant a place where you could walk forever on your grandfather's land and spend time with cousins. All the stories I had heard about social hardships and political oppression became more than family myth reading these narratives and for that I am thankful.

Throughout the process of studying these narratives I gained a tremendous amount of respect for one interviewer; Samuel S Taylor, whose empathetic and intelligent transcriptions popped out on the page to me even before I learned that he was one of only two black interviewers in the Arkansas section. His work changed the collection of transcripts in ways that I am still discovering, and allows all of us a more authentic, more realistic view of the difficult reality of the lives of these individuals. I am grateful for his skills.

I would like to acknowledge with deep gratitude the *National Endowment of the Arts for the Fellowship in Poetry*. The recognition it provided and the material assistance gave me a righteous boost to do the research and have the time to complete this book. Additionally, I would like to thank *the National Endowment for the Humanities,* whose support allowed me to attend *Don't Deny My Voice*, a seminar on Black poetry at the University of Kansas. I want to thank my editor Randall Horton, whose assistance and encouragement helped to write the book I really wanted to write. Additionally, I would like to thank Heather Buchanan for establishing a press that celebrates authentic intellectual inclusion. Also, I want to give a special thanks to Natalie Gerber and Tom Cable for their seminars on beat prosody and intonation at the *Poetry by The Sea Conference*. It provided a new gaze for me to see my work. Additionally, I am fortunate to have three colleagues: Maureen McDonnell, Rita Malenczyk, and Lauren Rosenberg that authentically define the term ally. I am grateful for their presence in my life. And finally, as in all things, much love and gratitude to my family: Carol, Ginny and Lucas—without whom none of this means anything.

Notes

Refugeed. This is a concept that occurs again and again in the slave narratives. Exactly how many slaves were "run" or "refugeed" to Texas during the war is difficult to say, though estimates range from 50,000 to 150,000 or more. If the estimates at the higher end of that range are accurate, then the number of slaves refugeed to Texas rivaled the number of black men who enlisted in the Union army during the War and would have increased the slave population of the state by 50 percent. (McDaniel, W. Caleb. (2014). "Remembering Henry: Refugeed Slaves in Civil War Texas." http://hdl.handle.net/1911/75992.)

Prologue

- *Transcription of the Slave Narrative by Henrietta Ralls*

    Ralls, Henrietta. ""Yes Ma'am, I Was Here in Slavery Times"" *Federal Writer's Project, United States Work Projects Administration (USWPA).* Source: *WPA Slave Narrative Project, Arkansas Narratives, Volume 2*, Manuscript Division, Library of Congress and Photographs Division, Library of Congress, 23 Mar. 2001. Web. 4 Apr. 2012.

    The Works Progress Administration (WPA) was the largest agency in Franklin D. Roosevelt's New Deal economic relief, reform, and recovery agenda during the Great Depression, as their "make-work" programs got millions of unemployed people back to work. One component of the WPA, the Federal Writers' Project (FWP), sponsored unemployed writers to undertake assorted research and writing assignments, including conducting oral history interviews of ex-slaves in the Southern and border states. By the time the program ended in 1939, Arkansas had generated the largest portion of the interviews, nearly one-third, now known collectively as the WPA Slave Narratives. (Spurgeon, John. "WPA Slave Narratives." *The Encyclopedia of Arkansas History & Culture.* The Central Arkansas Library System, 1 Nov. 2003. Web. 1 Apr. 2012.)

- *Driving Lesson*

The lines "survive on sadness" and "none of my tears are white" are from Gil Scot Heron

- *Supplementary Instructions #9-E To The American Guide Manual.* This can found in:

    USA. The Federal Writer's Project 1936-1938. Work Projects Administration. *Slave Narratives A Folk History of Slavery in the United States* From Interviews With Former Slaves. Washington: Library of Congress Project, 1941. Records of the Works Administration [WPA]. National Archives. Web. 11 July 2015.

I

- All of the original transcriptions of the slave narratives (both those used to make poems and those printed in full in the text) can be found at the following website.

    Born in Slavery: Slave Narratives from the Federal Writer's Project, 1936-1938. Manuscript Division, Library of Congress and Photographs Division, Library of Congress, 23 Mar. 2001. Web. 4 Apr. 2012. <Icweb2.loc.gov>.

Stealing Prayer	based on the transcribed narrative of Rachel Fairly
No Hoodoo	based on the transcribed narrative of Lucretia Alexander
Empty Pretty Land	based on the transcribed narrative of Doo Quin
Biscuit Dirt	based on the transcribed narrative of James Bertran
You Could Live	based on the transcribed narrative of Sallie Crane
Ash Cakes and Silence	based on the transcribed narrative of Richard Gum
New Onions Old Scars	based on the transcribed narrative of Henrietta Ral
Early Moon Gourd	based on the transcribed narrative of Lulu Jackson
Before Cotton Sacks and Cabins	based on the transcribed narrative of Mattie Aldridge
One Ear and Half a Face of Scars	based on the transcribed narrative of James Grahan

- *Free Raised.* This phrase occurs in several of the slave narratives. It seems to mean different things to different slaves that were raised in different regions. Here is how one slave Ellen Brass described it: "My father was free raised. The white folks raised him. I don't know how he became free. All that I know is that he was raised right in the house with the white folks and was free. His mother and father were both slaves. I was quite small at the time and didn't know much. They bought us like cattle and carried us from place to place." (Ellen Brass to Samuel S. Taylor May 11, 1938)

- *Interviewer Four* is based on the life and work of Samuel S. Taylor

- Copy of "*Notes by an Editor on Dialect Usage in Accounts by Interviews with Ex-Slaves.*" June 20, 1937. Prepared by Sterling A. Brown. This can be found in:

    USA. The Federal Writer's Project 1936-1938. Work Projects Administration. *Slave Narratives A Folk History of Slavery in the United State*s From Interviews

With Former Slaves. Washington: Library of Congress Project, 1941. Records of the Works Administration [WPA]. National Archives. Web. 11 July 2015.

- *Questions (Part 1,2,3)*

  All 72 lines in the six Question Excerpt poems are taken from the Questionnaire for Ex Slaves from the Roscoe Lewis Papers, Collie P. Huntington Library Hampton Institute, Hampton VA. Most of the questions are used as they appear with minor superficial edits to make them read as questions in semi-standard English. There were 333 questions in this version. You can find the original in:

  "Appendix 6." *Weevils in the Wheat: Interviews with Virginia Ex-Slaves*. Ed. Charles Perdue, Thomas Barden, and Robert Phillips. First Virginia Paperback Edition ed. Charlottesville: U of Virginia, 1976. 367. Print.

About the Author

Reginald Flood is a native of south central Los Angeles who now lives in a small town in southeastern Connecticut with his family. He is an associate professor of English and Coordinator of African American Studies at Eastern Connecticut State University, where he teaches African American literature and creative writing.

www.ingramcontent.com/pod-product-compliance
Lightning Source LLC
Chambersburg PA
CBHW030450010526
44118CB00011B/867